DISNEY AND THE BIBLE

Disney

and the Bible

A Scriptural Critique of the Magic Kingdom

Perucci Ferraiuolo

HORIZON BOOKS
CAMP HILL, PENNSYLVANIA

Horizon Books
3825 Hartzdale Drive
Camp Hill, PA 17011

ISBN: 0-88965-147-7
Mass market edition

97 98 99 00 01   5 4 3 2 1

Unless otherwise indicated, Scripture taken from
the HOLY BIBLE, Authorized King James Version.

"AND THE BIBLE" is a trademark of Horizon Books,
an imprint of Christian Publications, Inc.

All Walt Disney quotes presented at the beginning
of each chapter taken from *Wisdom Magazine:
The Journal of the Wisdom Society for the Advancement of Knowledge,*
vol. 32, December 1959.

Dedication

To Mom, Dad, Nani and Papa—you done good! And to my wife Babs, the crowning glory of this old war horse. Through dating, marriage, childbirth, motherhood and a partnership authored by the Most High, you have been my inspiration, balance, sounding board and unequivocal supporter of every word I write and every thought I perceive. When I tire, you invigorate; when I become downtrodden, you inspire; and when I succeed, you are the gentle reminder that all good things come from above.

Table of Contents

Foreword

This book is a first! Hats off to Perry Ferraiuolo for almost "risking his life" to call into question and challenge the morality level of the current Disney empire. The book is needed, accurate and practical. It's like a trumpet blast of warning, alerting millions who are being sucked down the horrible drain of lewdness, slowly but surely.

Whether it's the subtle sex of *Pretty Woman*, the rawness of *Pulp Fiction* or the perverted nature of *Priest*, all of his examples point out one thing—the ship of decency and morality is slowly (or maybe not so slowly) sinking.

One thing is clear: Ferraiuolo is right—"The days of Ward and June Cleaver are over!" He's right again in saying that when Walt Disney died, something very special died with him. Even the "other side" of Disney was mild compared with what the company is producing today.

The author has done a commendable job of accuracy in describing what has really happened. The chapter titled "Mickey Comes Out of the Closet" is controversial to be sure, but very powerfully done, and done with accuracy. He points out, sadly, the strong ties the corporation has with the homosexual agenda, basically just to be politically correct.

This book will be like a hurricane-force wind. It will pull up what isn't morally and biblically nailed down. I, for one, am grateful for men like Perry Ferraiuolo who call it like it is. His direct quotes from Walt Disney himself are worth the price of the book!

Bob Moorehead
Author and Senior Pastor
Overlake Christian Church
Kirkland, Washington

Preface

It was Saturday night; I was nine years old and on my way to the drive-in theater with Mom, Dad and my three sisters, packed inside our brand new salmon-pink 1955 Ford station wagon.

The excitement was so thick you could touch it. We were on our way to see Walt Disney's *Lady and the Tramp*. It was an electrifying experience to see one of the top movies of the day with the whole family.

Dad went to the snack bar for the usual—lots of buttered popcorn, candy and soda pop. And Mom would always remind him to bring napkins, but he almost never did. It didn't matter, though. We were a family doing what most families did every time a Disney film premiered—go to see it.

I remember laughing at the antics of *Lady and the Tramp,* crying when Old Yeller died, taking a lot of ribbing when Perri the Squirrel debuted (since that's my name, albeit spelled differently) and sitting mesmerized while the Shaggy Dog romped across the screen. I believed that a kiss could awaken a princess after seeing *Sleeping Beauty,* and I wanted to be Davy Crockett so bad it hurt. To this day, one of my most prized possessions is an original, mint condition Davy Crockett knife.

There was no other word for it but *magical*. It was a time of tight family union, a time of family-oriented films that charmed us and entertained us by appealing to our innocence. Disney films made kids feel ten feet tall and adults feel like Peter Pan.

We watched awe-inspiring documentaries like *Men Against the Arctic* and *The Living Desert*; high-adventure films like *20,000 Leagues Under the Sea* and *Kidnapped*; side-splitting comedies like *The Parent Trap* and *The Absent-Minded Professor*; and ever-popular cartoons like *Pinocchio*, *Dumbo*, *Bambi*, *Fantasia*, *Snow White and the Seven Dwarfs* and *Cinderella*. To kids like me, growing up under the shadow of those famous mouse ears, having Walt Disney around was like having another father. We trusted him, believed in him and wanted to be just like the characters he created.

I remember tucking my Davy Crockett knife into my waistband, donning a coonskin cap my grandmother bought me and mounting an arm of our couch, pretending it was Davy's trusty steed. With my imaginary sidekick, Georgie Russell (who coincidentally looked a lot like Buddy Ebsen, the original actor who played Russell), a broom handle that served as a flintlock rifle and two folded towels that made quite a nice saddle, I would play for hours, retracing Davy's heroic, Indian-fighter steps from Washington, D.C. to the Alamo.

I can still hear the anthem as I proudly rode that couch horse: "Born on a mountaintop in Tennessee; greatest state in the land of the free. . . . Davy, Davy Crockett, king of the wild frontier."

How I loved those days! We refer to them as the innocent fifties, the days of Ward and June Cleaver or just the good ole days—when you didn't have to sell your car to afford to go to the movies.

But something happened when the heart of the creator of Mickey Mouse stopped beating on December 15, 1966—the result of acute circulatory collapse. America lost much more than just a brilliant and beloved animator; in some ways, the nation, if not the world, lost its innocence when Walt Disney died.

Acknowledgments

My continuing respect and friendship goes to Rolly Devore—one of the most thorough and detailed researchers in the industry. His precision, enlightenment and startling discoveries only augment the fact that no book is an individual effort. His nickname as the "Sanctified Bloodhound" for absolute truth is well suited.

But there were others whose immeasurable commitment to this book is the real reason it is in print today. First, my wife Babs, whose boot-in-the-backside anointing kept me spilling ink when I wanted to soak in the hot tub; my daughter, Megan, who managed to understand that passion for prose is sometimes heard as a growl, and who learned to brew Sumatra coffee like a pro; and last but not least my son Benjamin, who kept my office well stocked with dinosaurs, Hot Wheels, police cars and Legos—all given with love and caring to help carry me through to the end. It all worked!

And also to the publishers, who exhibited the stability of Paul, the puissance of David and the forbearance of Job while experiencing author eccentricities and re-edits of the re-edits. Their commitment to this book remains an archetype for all other publishers to emulate.

Introduction

He was the single most impactful human being in film animation and children's entertainment. To the world, he was the creator of the child in all of us—animating, directing and producing films, cartoons, documentaries and musicals that brought literally hundreds of millions of fans to the theaters in search of wholesome entertainment that was suitable for the entire family. It was what they had always come to expect from the man whose international symbol was the Fantasyland castle.

But the headlines and feelings about Disney's company have changed. Once trusted and applauded for uncompromising movies that proudly carried the "G" rating, the Hollywood machine started by Uncle Walt (as he was dubbed by countless fans) suddenly began to crank out movies that would outrage over three generations of Disney devotees.

Movies like *Priest* and *The Hand That Rocks the Cradle*[1] shocked millions, and sexually laced, suggestive, subliminal and/or morally questionable animated features like *The Lion King*, *Aladdin*, *The Little Mermaid* and others have virtually ripped the heart out of the once-lauded Magic Kingdom. To many, the Disney corporation became "the mouse that roared," but with new and astounding revelations about the current Disney attitude, it appears that Uncle Walt's family haven has become troubled with an agenda that includes sexual immorality, homosexuality, violence and antifamily productions.

To understand what the Disney conglomerate has become, it is crucial to look at what it used to be and at the person who became "Hollywood's family man."

The Man Behind the Legend

Walt Disney was born in Chicago on December 5, 1901 and at the age of fourteen enrolled at the Kansas City Art Institute. Less than two years later, in the declining months of World War I, he volunteered as a Red Cross ambulance driver. After landing stateside again, he went to work at a Kansas City art studio where he met fellow artist Ub Iwerks, the man who would become Disney's lifelong friend, partner and collaborator.

The duo teamed up to make animated commercials, but quickly graduated to cartoons, which they sold to theaters under their hastily put together company, Laugh-O-Grams.

Disney was so delighted with the cartoons and their acceptance that he jumped full speed into his first production company, also called Laugh-O-Grams. Soon after he faced his first financial disaster, but certainly not his last. The venture ended in bankruptcy.

His dream intact, Disney headed for Hollywood, and in 1923 formed a partnership with his brother Roy and Iwerks, which produced his first series of live-action cartoons called *Alice in Cartoonland*.

From there, the fledgling production company released Oswald Rabbit (1927) and in 1928 created Mickey Mouse. Though the first two Mouse adventures were silent (in both speech and acceptance), Disney displayed his never-say-die temperament and premiered his third Mouse cartoon, *Steamboat Willie*, with the addition of sound. Walt himself provided the high-pitched voice for the rodent and tasted his first nibble of Hollywood success.

From there, Disney released its Silly Symphony cartoon series, complete with pre-recorded musical track. In that series lurked the best known and most successful, *The Three Little Pigs* (1933), which introduced the monster hit song, "Who's Afraid of the Big Bad Wolf?"

A Hollywood Phenomenon

Disney was on a roll. With Mickey Mouse and *The Three Little Pigs* running around garnering success for the animator, a whole zoo full of characters came to life, including Mickey's future wife Minnie, Goofy, Donald Duck and Pluto.

Boasting a veritable stable of animated stars,

the Disney organization quickly grew into a major Hollywood phenomenon. The studio was employing hundreds of people and realizing tremendous profits from the merchandising of products spawned from its cartoon characters, but Disney was willing to risk it all on a never-before-attempted venture: a full-length animated feature.

The result was the tremendously successful *Snow White and the Seven Dwarfs*. Soon thereafter, Disney tried it again with *Fantasia*, a project which not only received enormous critical acclaim but also gave Walt his first taste of public rage and controversy.

At first a huge financial calamity that threatened to destroy Disney, *Fantasia* combined animation with classical music on a scale that had never been attempted before. Music purists were outraged, calling the film a vulgarization of classical music through popular imagery. And some family and church groups worried that depictions of characters like the Demon of Bald Mountain, Mickey Mouse as a sorcerer, and the Pegasus Family (featured in the Pastoral Symphony) would conjure up nightmares for kids, or even promote black magic. (*Fantasia* is discussed in more detail in a later chapter.)

Shortly after *Fantasia*, Disney's animators went on strike, saying that Walt Disney was authoritarian and played favorites. There was a mass exodus of talent but, as would be the norm, Disney would survive—and thrive.

In response to the strike, Walt offered a twenty-six-page reply, saying in part:

> This business is ready to go ahead. If you want to go ahead with it . . . you've got to be ready for some hard work. . . . If the business is to survive the many storms that are ahead of it, it must be made strong; and that strength comes from the individual strength of the employees. Don't forget this—it's the law of the universe that the strong shall survive and the weak must fall by the way; and I don't give a [expletive deleted] what idealistic plan is cooked up, nothing can change that.[2]

The Other Side of Disney

According to many sources, Walt Disney wasn't above intimidating the union bosses and their rank and file animators. At one point, he announced to the media that he was so thrilled with his jump into live-action (i.e., *The Reluctant Dragon*) that he was planning on dropping animation altogether in favor of live-action movies.[3]

This move outraged friend and foe alike, but Walt wasn't finished yet. He allegedly called a press conference and publicly auditioned his loyal band of ever-faithful females who worked for the studio. In one of the most bizarre moments of his career, Disney encouraged his girls to show up in skimpy bathing suits for his personal perusal. On that day dozens of the studio's hopeful "Hollywood honeys" displayed their charms to their leering boss and an equally leering press. Publicity photos revealed a previously unseen side of Disney that shocked the public and dismayed his brother and partner, Roy.[4]

During the strike, Walt also showed an all-consuming vindictiveness toward those who opposed him. When one top animator and strike leader jeered at him (much to the approval of the other strikers) as he drove through his studio gates one morning, Disney allegedly jumped out of his car, tore off his jacket and lunged for the man. After being restrained by his own security guards, Disney told the artist that he was through, not just at Disney but everywhere in the industry.

Once in his office, though, Disney arranged to have a photographer take pictures of the men out on the picket line. They were delivered that afternoon, and he papered the walls of his office with them, after which he walked around the room pointing out individuals to his brother Roy that he thought would have remained loyal. "[Expletive deleted], I didn't think he'd go against me," he said about one; about another, "That [expletive deleted], I trusted him and he went out on me." As for a third, he shrugged and said, "We can get along without him."[5]

Many say that Disney the artist and animator often collided with Disney the powerful, almost ruthless studio head, but at the end of each battle emerged a creativity that has remained unequaled in the industry.

A Corporate Heritage?

Perhaps Walt Disney's legend and lore, along with his penchant for perfection and cold, corporate behavior, have been unwittingly passed on to Michael Eisner. Eisner turned Disney into a money-making machine, an achievement that has earned the applause of the entertainment industry and stockholders. But in the process he has fashioned it into a haven churning out anti-family and anti-Christian movies for the sake of money, prestige and all-encompassing power.

Endnotes

1. It should be noted that there is a distinct difference between Disney the man, Disney the corporation, Disney the studio, Disney the film production company, Disney the record company, Disney the book publisher and Disney the theme park operator. In most cases, "Disney," as used in this book, is an all-encompassing term referring to the entire Disney empire. Movies such as *Priest* and *The Hand That Rocks the Cradle*, though not produced by Disney itself, are produced by Disney subsidiaries like Miramax and Hollywood Pictures, specifically relegated to produce what the Disney organization calls "adult" motion pictures, since the entertainment conglomerate was

and is desirous of protecting its alleged family film image.

2. Richard Holliss and Brian Sibley, *The Disney Studio Story* (New York: Crown Publishers, 1988), pp. 43-44.

3. Marc Eliot, *Walt Disney: Hollywood's Dark Prince* (New York: Carol Publishing, 1993), p. 139.

4. Ibid.

5. Ibid., p. 142.

What the Bible Says about Bringing Up Children

And, ye fathers, provoke not your children to wrath: but bring them up in the nurture and admonition of the Lord. (Ephesians 6:4)

Fathers, provoke not your children to anger, lest they be discouraged. (Colossians 3:21)

Train up a child in the way he should go: and when he is old, he will not depart from it. (Proverbs 22:6)

Therefore shall ye lay up these my words in your heart and in your soul. . . . And ye shall teach them your children, speaking of them when thou sittest in thine house, and when thou walkest by the way, when thou liest down, and when thou risest up. (Deuteronomy 11:18-19)

The rod and reproof give wisdom: but a child left to himself bringeth his mother to shame. (Proverbs 29:15)

He [Amaziah] did according to all things as Joash his father did. (2 Kings 14:3)

And the Lord said to Samuel, . . . For I have told him that I will judge his house for ever for the iniquity which he knoweth; because his sons made themselves vile, and he restrained them not. (1 Samuel 3:11, 13)

Chapter 1

The Goddess of the Forties

Nothing is ever born afraid. . . . Young things—human and animal—boy or black lamb—have had no experience with fear. They rely implicitly on parents—on something bigger and stronger than themselves to assure safety. . . . On God as they grow older and threats to security multiply.
                                        —Walt Disney

By the 1930s Walt Disney was hot. His cartoons, with Mickey Mouse at the helm, were pouring money into the studio's coffers. But the same mouse that brought the Disney dream together also tore it apart.

It all began when Disney premiered Mickey's predecessor, Oswald Rabbit. Through some fairly bad negotiations, Disney lost the rights to Oswald. On the train ride back to Hollywood, Disney hit upon the notion of a new cartoon character. Inspiration came by way of a real mouse that used to live in his old Kansas City office during his Laugh-O-Gram days.

Mickey Is Born

Walt told of Mickey's birth in this way: "Mice gathered in my wastebasket when I worked late at night," he said. "I lifted them out and kept them in little cages on my desk. One of them was my particular friend."[1]

Disney legend says that by the time he got back to Hollywood, Walt had drawn Mickey on a piece of paper. He even had the plot worked out for the very first Mickey Mouse cartoon.

Other available records dispute that version. Dave Iwerks, son of Walt's partner, Ub Iwerks, says Mickey's journey from conception to reality took a less than truthful spin at the hands of Disney.

"It's pretty clear now that Mickey was Ub's character," Dave says. "Even the Disney archives concede that Ub created Mickey, although their version has it that Walt stood over Ub's shoulder when he did it. The whole scenario of the train story the studio used to be so fond of is just not right at all."[2]

Disney did not even name Mickey. Walt wanted to call him Mortimer, but Walt's wife, Lillian, said it sounded "too sissy." She suggested Mickey, and Walt went along with it.

According to Dave Iwerks, Walt Disney had

only the vaguest idea for a new cartoon character. He and Ub independently sketched their ideas on character sheets. When Walt showed Ub his version of the mouse, Ub rejected it, saying it looked too much like Walt. Disney then confessed he had used his own face as a model.

Taking several drawings of Oswald Rabbit, Ub changed the ears a bit, rounded the eyes and turned him into Mickey.

Disney allegedly laughed when he saw how easily they could steal Oswald back from the people who stole him in the first place. And Disney learned firsthand just how the big-time movie industry operated.[3]

In the weeks that followed, Iwerks also learned something. At the time, he was producing over 700 individual Mickey Mouse drawings a day. And Walt took all the credit for drawing the mouse. Tension between the two creative masters heightened. It was the demise of a productive working relationship and a longtime friendship.

"My father felt overlooked and underappreciated at Disney," Dave recounts. "He'd begun as a partner and was now an employee."

When a competitor gave Ub the chance to start his own studio, he jumped at it. In a short period of time Disney lost his best friend, his distributor, his music director and $150,000 of urgently needed royalty payments—something he never quite recovered from.[4]

It is quite clear that, early on, Disney had

trouble with relationships. His authoritarian way and ego had pushed many inkers, studio hands and top animators into other studios; he had extensive problems communicating with his wife Lillian; and he felt betrayed when his brother Roy announced that he was getting married.[5]

Disney, it seems, as with many of us, suffered greatly because of damaged relationships through sins of commission or omission. Bible teacher and former editor Tom Marshall puts it this way: "Relationships can gather stress and begin to flounder either because we persist in doing things that hurt the relationship or because we fail to do the things that are necessary to keep it alive and well.

"The trouble is," he continues, "that sins of omission are hard to recognize and harder still for us to admit. Our conscience, for example, is not very sensitive to the things we don't do that we should do. It is much more effective at pointing out the things we are doing that we should not be doing."[6]

Marshall says that relationships are damaged by breaches of trust—suspicion, disloyalty, dishonesty, moral weakness and thoughtlessness. In several key areas there can be no doubt that Disney breached the trust, though somewhat unwittingly, of Iwerks and a whole laundry list of animators, studio extras, musicians, directors and writers who, once loyal to Disney, now deserted him and his dreams. Disney, they felt, was a cold, hard, calculated, authoritarian taskmaster.

A Difficult Past

But as so often is the case, Disney seems to have learned his behavior from his father. Both Walt and older brother Roy were forced to toil on their farm to earn their keep, and their father Elias used physical punishment and authoritarian discipline to reach optimum productivity. According to reports, the elder Disney's punishment was brutal. Disney researcher Marc Eliot paints a heart-rending picture:

> In the evenings, following a beating, Walt would often lie awake in bed whimpering. Roy, older and physically stronger, was able to endure the punishments better than his little brother. He would rub Walt's hurts and rock him to sleep with promises that everything would be all right in the morning. Walt would bury his head in the bend of Roy's elbow and ask if the man who beat them was really his father or just some mean old man who looked like him and wanted only to frighten him.
>
> On the rare days he wasn't punished, Walt looked forward to that part of the evening when, after he had gone to bed, his mother would read fairy tales to him in her soothing, expressive voice until he slipped gently into sleep.
>
> Often he would fall asleep huddled

close to Roy. . . . Other times, during the day, Walt would sneak into his mother's bedroom and put her clothes on and her makeup. Afterward, he would stand in front of her full-length mirror to admire his reflection.[7]

There was also the question of Walt Disney's parentage. After Walt graduated from high school, he tried to enlist in the army. When a local recruiter asked to see his birth certificate, Disney wrote Chicago's Cook County Hall of Records only to find that there was no record of his birth. He then contacted his church, but again there were no records. He asked his father about it, who told him it was all a mistake and that he would find the birth certificate. He never did.

According to Eliot, this disturbed Disney greatly.

Why wasn't there an accurate record of his birth? What secrets, if any, were his parents hiding from him? Would they ever tell him? Could he ever be sure what they said was the truth? The only thing he was certain of was that he wasn't certain of anything, except that he no longer felt he could trust his parents and wouldn't again from that time on. This infection of doubt would eat at Walt the rest of his days, infusing his future films with a feverish passion that would deepen their dramatic themes.[8]

Eliot cites the stepchild abandoned in the woods in *Snow White*; the puppet in *Pinocchio* who longs to be Geppetto's real son; the little creature in *Bambi* who loses his mother; the sorcerer's apprentice in fearful servitude in *Fantasia*; the baby elephant separated from his mother in *Dumbo*. "All [the films] have in common their main characters' quests to find their real parents."[9]

To a great extent, Walt was abused and ridiculed by his father—or by the man who supposedly was his father. Where there should have been protection, there was emotional desertion. Where there might have been nurturing, there was cruelty. Where there could have been positive bonding, there was a rift that Walt could not overcome.

With his failing health and business inadequacies, Elias Disney seemed to vent his frustrations by physically and emotionally hurting Walt. When Walt needed reassurance in the face of family crisis, his father only beat him time and time again.

So the questions could easily be posed to Walt Disney: Why did you rule your empire with an authoritarian hand? Why did you scold, intimidate and even humiliate your employees? Why did you set yourself up as a cruel taskmaster? The answer seems to howl like an icy wind: *I just did what I saw my father do.*

Disney, though, did something his father never did. He succeeded in the face of a devastating childhood, a poor economy and extreme resistance from the Hollywood power structure.

Myths and Movies

After a series of tremendously successful short cartoons, and with Mickey Mouse garnering increasing success and profits for "Uncle Walt," as he was now called, Disney turned his sights to something never done before—the production of a feature-length cartoon. Entitled *Snow White*, the critics dubbed it "Disney's Folly."

Undaunted, Walt surged ahead, even though he knew full well that his animators had little or no experience drawing human characters. In order to hone their collective talent in that direction, he decided to produce another of his popular "Silly Symphony" shorts entitled *The Goddess of Spring*, based on the Greek goddess Persephone. Though a mythical character, Persephone was required to move and perform as a live actress would, conveying wide-ranging subtleties of emotion.[10]

The introduction of Greek mythology into Disney's works was a precursor to his embracing a wide range of antibiblical themes, including black magic, witchcraft, sorcery and mysticism.

In *The Goddess of Spring*, the story line centers around Persephone, the daughter of Demeter, considered the caretaker of the earth. Legend has it that when Demeter and Persephone walked through a garden, even the evening primroses opened up just to watch them pass by.

Another god, Pluto, was not so fortunate. He didn't rule the heavens or the earth. He ruled the kingdom of the dead, deep within the dark, bitter-cold earth.

Pluto searched the universe for a wife, but no one wanted to give up the sunshine and flowers of the earth to live in his dark domain. So he kidnapped Persephone, even though the trees shouted to her, "Come back!" and to Pluto, "Leave her alone!"

Demeter was distraught. She thought of nothing else but to find her daughter. As a result, the crops stopped growing and the flowers wilted. As Demeter wept, the trees wept with her, shedding their leaves in brown and yellow tears.

Demeter found out from the rivers that Persephone was kidnapped by Pluto and was living in the underworld. So she made the journey to Mount Olympus and begged almighty Zeus to do something.

Zeus was concerned. If Demeter continued the way she was, the crops would fail and the trees and flowers would dry up and die. The "little people" on the earth, he surmised, would stop paying tribute to him. He just had to intervene.

So mighty Zeus sent the god Hermes to rescue Persephone. There was one consideration. If Persephone ate anything while in the underworld, she could not be rescued.

By the time Hermes and Demeter got to Pluto and Persephone, Pluto had persuaded Persephone to eat. Out of twelve pomegranate seeds he gave her, she had eaten six. When this word reached Zeus, he had to make a quick decision.

"Because Persephone ate six of the twelve seeds, let her live for six months of every year in the kingdom of the dead," Zeus said. "For the other six months let her live with her mother on the earth. And let no one argue with the judgment of Zeus!"

That is why in the summertime the flowers bloom, the grass is green and the trees wear blossoms, then leaves, then fruit. Demeter, you see, is rushing happily here and there, tending the earth like a garden.

But in the autumn, Persephone travels down to the underworld to keep her bargain with Pluto. First she learned to pity him, but then she learned to love him. Up on the earth, however, Demeter misses her daughter, so the trees flush red with calling Persephone's name, then drop their leaves. The flowers wither and the crops stop growing. The earth and the people on it anxiously wait for Persephone to return with the spring.[11]

The Goddess of Spring wasn't a big success at the box office, and likely not with Bible-believing Christians, who know who created the earth and who continues to care for it and for what reasons.

The First Full-Length Film

The picture, nevertheless, gave Disney's animators the experience they needed, and Disney pushed on to finish *Snow White and the Seven Dwarfs*, the story of the little princess who runs away from her wicked stepmother and seeks refuge with seven little men in a woodland cottage. One of the world's best-loved fairy-tales, it's an old story that, through hundreds of retellings, has become a part of the nursery mythology of Britain and North America.[12]

Yet for all its winsomeness and charm, the cuddly, funny, floppy dwarfs of *Snow White* are deeply rooted in mystic lore. In folk legends and fairy tales, dwarfs were always described as creatures of small stature, ranging from the size of a man's thumb to the height of a two-year-old child.

In appearance and feelings, they roughly resembled human beings. But magical powers endowed them with special skills and wisdom far beyond those of human mortals. Inhabiting the dark and secret places of the earth, dwarfs could appear or disappear with bewildering rapidity.

These mischievous and sometimes malicious beings teased farm animals and abducted children and beautiful maidens. They stole bread and corn. They became the omnipotent lords of the mine where they labored for the common good of other dwarfs.

Mythology suggests that the kind of toiling

dwarfs depicted in *Snow White* either came to life as dark maggots crawling from the decaying flesh of the slain giant Ymir or from the scarlet billows of the seas formed by the same giant's blood. The gods supposedly granted them the wits and shape of men and gave the more celestial of them the duty of upholding the four corners of the sky.[13]

As quickly as Disney embraced *Snow White,* he wholeheartedly welcomed *Pinocchio,* one of Disney's most enduring classics. It was terrifyingly crafted with images so startling that whole generations of children have been captivated by it.

The movie opens with Jiminy Cricket, as the conscience of Pinocchio, singing the Oscar-winning song, "When You Wish Upon a Star" as he sits on a book entitled *Pinocchio.*

The cricket then guides us to Geppetto's little toy shop. The wood carver is just finishing painting a smile on his newest puppet, a little boy named Pinocchio.

That night, as the old man is about to fall asleep, he sees the Wishing Star through an open window and wishes Pinocchio could be a real, human boy. As Geppetto sleeps, the Blue Fairy descends from the Wishing Star and grants Geppetto's desire. The wooden Pinocchio can run and talk and act like a live boy. The fairy promises Pinocchio that if he is brave and unselfish and learns right from wrong, he will find himself transformed into a real flesh-and-blood boy.

Throughout the rest of the movie, Pinocchio

gets into about as much trouble as any real live boy can. Something like the Jonah of the Bible, Pinocchio ends up in the belly of a whale. And, like Jonah, he survives the ordeal and becomes a real live boy.

Noted film reviewer Roger Ebert thinks Pinocchio is plausible to the average kid—unlike Disney's *The Little Mermaid*. "Kids may not understand falling in love with a prince," says Ebert in one of his reviews, "but they understand not listening to your father and being a bad boy and running away and getting into real trouble."[14]

Endnotes

1. Marc Eliot, *Walt Disney: Hollywood's Dark Prince* (New York: Carol Publishing, 1993), p. 36.

2. Ibid.

3. Ibid.

4. Ibid., pp. 56-57.

5. Ron Carlson and Ed Decker, *Fast Facts on False Teachings* (Eugene, OR: Harvest House, 1994), pp. 246-257.

6. Tom Marshall, *Right Relationships* (Chichester, England: Sovereign World, 1988), p. 67.

7. Eliot, p. 48.

8. Ibid., p. 12.

9. Marc Eliot, "The Dark Side of Uncle Walt," *Los Angeles Magazine,* Vol. 38, No. 5, May 1993, p. 48.

10. Richard Holliss and Brian Sibley, *The Disney Studio Story* (New York: Crown Books, 1988), p. 28.

11. Geraldine McCaughrean, *Greek Myths* (New York: Macmillan Publishing, 1992), pp. 15-20.

12. Holliss and Sibley, p. 26.

13. Marshall Cavendish, *Man, Myth and Magic,* Vol. 3 (New York: Marshall Cavendish, 1995), pp. 734-737.

14. *Microsoft Cinemania '95* (Redmond, WA: Microsoft, 1995), compact disc.

What the Bible Says about Sorcery

Thou shalt not suffer a witch to live. (Exodus 22:18)

There shall not be found among you any one that . . . useth divination, or an observer of times, or an enchanter, or a witch, or a charmer, or a consulter with familiar spirits, or a wizard, or a necromancer. For all that do these things are an abomination unto the LORD. *(Deuteronomy 18:10-12)*

For without [the heavenly city] *are dogs, and* **sorcerers,** *and whoremongers, and murderers, and idolaters, and whosoever loveth and maketh a lie. (Revelation 22:15,* emphasis added)

But refuse profane and old wives' fables, and exercise thyself rather unto godliness. (1 Timothy 4:7)

Chapter 2

Sorcerers, Demons and Obsession

The motion picture has become one of the marvels of all time; a true Wonder of the World in its magical powers. But what is wrought on the screen for every man and his family to see and ponder has been even more wonderful.

—*Walt Disney*

If there was one film that epitomized the anti-biblical theme running through some of Disney's early works, it was the 1940 release of *Fantasia*—an almost total glorification of witchcraft, sorcery and satanism set to classical music.

Adorning the film were a veritable menagerie of centaurs (in Greek mythology, a half-man, half-horse creature descended from Ixion), centaurettes, fauns (baby centaurs complete with cranial horns) and water nymphs (in Greek mythology, a form of female divinity, immortal or long-lived, associated with various natural objects or places and regarded as young, beautiful, musical and sexually amorous). There were also unicorns, vulcans (gods of fire), demons, Chernobog (in Slavic mythology, a god of malignant evil) and a bevy of malificent evil spirits, demons and grotesque fiends—the complete antithesis of the God of the Bible.

Just a description of the various sections in the movie may cause some to question how or why Disney marketed this film to children. For example, Cinebooks' *Motion Picture Guide Review*, in labeling *Fantasia* as a revolutionary integration of great works and wonderfully imaginative animated visuals, illustrates perhaps the most famous section in the movie, "The Sorcerer's Apprentice":

> When the old sorcerer goes to bed, Mickey Mouse, the title character, tires of carrying buckets of water and scrubbing the floor, so he tries on the conjurer's tall conical hat (which glows slightly to suggest its magical properties) and commands a broom to grow arms and legs and tote the buckets. As Mickey watches the broom tirelessly fetching, he nods off, awakening from his dreams to find the room half-filled with water. He feverishly tries to stop the broom, but it will not obey him.

When he grabs an ax and chops the broom to pieces, each piece grows arms and legs and continues the task, although they are now completely submerged. The sorcerer appears at the top of the stairs and with a wave of his hand restores the room. With the slightest trace of suppressed amusement, he retrieves his broom from the sheepish Mickey, then gives the mouse a swat across the backside with it.[1]

Twisting the Sacred

In an affront to Roman Catholics, "Ave Maria"—Schubert's classic song tribute to Mary, the mother of Jesus—is one of the most touching and beautiful songs of all time, yet Disney chose to use it in the section of *Fantasia* called "Night on Bald Mountain," in which evil spirits rise from a graveyard and fly through the night to the mountaintop where Chernobog, the "black god," waits for them to pay homage to him. As the spirits swirl around him, Chernobog, who resembles a fusion of Dracula with a cow head, revels in his mastery of the underworld. As the dawn breaks, the spirits return to the graveyard and Chernobog retreats back inside the mountain. As he does so, in true Draculian fashion, strains of "Ave Maria" are heard in the background.

Though it seems malevolent in and of itself, this section of *Fantasia* is more than a mere conjuring up of make-believe. In the original Latin, the lyrics to "Ave Maria," which even Protestants could appreciate, are as follows: "Ave Maria, gratia plena, Dominus tecum. Benedicta tu in mulieribus, et benedictus fructus ventris tui Jesus."[2] Translated exactly, it means, "Hail Mary, full of grace, the Lord is with thee. Blessed art thou among women, and blessed is the fruit of thy womb, Jesus"—virtually the exact greeting Elizabeth gave Mary after Elizabeth's unborn son, John the Baptist, leaped in her womb at the very presence of the mother of the Son of God (Luke 1:39-45).

How ironic that a celebration of evil, such as *Fantasia*'s "Night on Bald Mountain" presents, is scored with a song that glorifies the One who defeated the very demon the movie promotes and glorifies.

In the late 1960s, *Fantasia* became a cult film for the hippie generation of druggies, many of whom believed that the entire Disney staff must have been high when they made it. Arthur Babbitt, the animator responsible for some of the movie said, "Yes, it is true. I myself was addicted to Ex-Lax and Feenamint."[3]

Disney biographer Richard Schickel says there were several low points in *Fantasia* besides the Bald Mountain sequence. Some critics, for example, panned the movie's creation-of-the-world scenes. The garish volcanic eruptions, with their evolutionary overtones, seemed out of place when set to Stravinsky's "Rite of Spring."[4]

Schickel goes on to comment about the film:

> To make sure everyone got the idea that this was art, the girl centaurs were originally drawn bare-breasted, but the Hays office insisted on discreet garlands being hung around their necks. The torsos and heads that topped the horse bodies of these creatures belonged to adolescent girls styled to resemble the teenager down the street.
>
> The sequence ends with the most explicit statement of anality ever made by the studio, which found in the human backside not only the height of humor but the height of sexuality as well. Two of the little cupids who scamper incessantly throughout the sequence finally draw a curtain over the scene. When they come together, their shiny little behinds form, for an instant, a heart.[5]

Disney, though, may have wanted the Bald Mountain scene in *Fantasia* for other than artistic reasons. According to Schickel, Disney was riddled with obsessions, one of which was a preoccupation with death.

Dark Predictions

Reportedly, at a party a fortuneteller predicted Disney would not live past his thirty-fifth birthday, a prediction that haunted him even after he passed that date. At best, he figured he'd been given a short reprieve, and for the rest of his days he avoided funerals and, when forced to attend, fell into long, brooding depressions.[6]

Disney even avoided reporters who wanted to write his story. His logic: Biographies are only written about dead people. According to Schickel, Disney worried that such reporters would pry into business and personal secrets (he saw little difference between the two). Moreover, they might somehow reverse the usual order of things, thereby causing his demise.[7]

There can be little doubt that Disney's occultic incursions in *Fantasia* and other films containing satanic teachings made him vulnerable to the whims and wiles of the spiritist he eventually encountered at the party. The fortuneteller's prediction affected him more, perhaps, than any other single incident.

Fortunetelling as part of the occult is directly forbidden by the Bible. In their book *Fast Facts on False Teachings*, Ron Carlson and Ed Decker deem fortunetelling deadly:

> God speaks clearly about the area of fortune-telling. Modern-day prophets and prophetesses claim to predict the events to come in your life and in the nation. But God in His Word gives us two tests to determine a true prophet. The first test is found in Deuteronomy

18:20-22. The prophecy must be tested. Does the prophecy come true or not? If it does not come true, you know that the prophet is not of God. The Hebrew prophets of the Old Testament were 100 percent accurate when they spoke from God, or they were stoned to death.[8]

The second test that God gives us to determine a true prophet is found in Deuteronomy 13:1-5. You must test the teaching. Are these prophets leading you to the worship of the true and living God? Even if the prophecy comes true, you must test the teaching by the Word of God, as Second Timothy 3:16-17 instructs.[9]

Marc Eliot says that Disney's absorption with his own death was a contributing factor in popularizing a huge three-part series hit for him: "Davy Crockett."

Walt looked to his personal angels and demons to produce a remarkable work of entertainment. No doubt, to Disney, Crockett's appeal lay in his single-minded fundamentalist commitment to American virtue, at least in Walt's version, where the life of the frontiersman/politician/patriot was sanitized and idealized. Disney's Crockett was forever the stoic whose most often-repeated line in the series, "Be sure you're right, then go ahead," became yet another of Walt's externalized alter egos.[10]

With just three episodes and a dead hero at the Alamo, Disney's Crockett took the world by storm. Many felt that Davy Crockett was even bigger than Mickey Mouse. There is, however, a unique twist to the Crockett story. Eliot adds this interesting postscript:

> Because the series ran over the course of several weeks, it would have been easy for Walt to change the last scene of the last episode and have Davy live. More than likely, it was Walt's obsession with his own aging and death that dictated his glorifying depiction of alter-ego Crockett's premature passage through the heavenly gates.[11]

Embellishing Tradition

One of Disney's best animated fairy tales remains *Cinderella*—a tale true to the original traditional story with a few comic embellishments, including Gus and Jaq, the mice who befriend Cinderella during her trials and tribulations at the hands of fate.

While there have been over 500 different versions of this fairy tale throughout the world, the most widely known and accepted version comes from a seventeenth-century French rendering.

Succinctly, *Cinderella* is the story of a poor, downtrodden girl, who becomes the victim of a cruel stepmother, but appears before her Prince Charming in a gorgeous disguise given her by her supernatural helper, her fairy godmother.

Untrue to the original ninth-century Chinese version, though, French author, Charles Perrault, added some details of his own to the story, which remain as part and parcel of the original legend.

Not invented by Disney by any stretch of the imagination, Perrault came up with the idea of the glass slipper, the pumpkin coach and the concept that Cinderella had to leave the ball by midnight when her magic finery would revert to rags.[12]

Perrault not only embellished the story with inventions of his own, he also omitted some of the important points found in the folk-tale versions.

In those, the heroine is usually helped by her dead mother, or by agents sent by her mother, and the prince carries off a false bride, who is denounced by a bird. And, in most of the folk versions, Cinderella receives supernatural help from a domesticated animal—a cow or a sheep—who is often her dead mother reincarnated. Perrault changed this animal into a fairy godmother, a curious half-pagan, half-Christian conception that Disney embraced for his version.[13]

At the end of the fairy tale, Cinderella shows a

Christian forgiveness toward her stepsisters, and even marries them off to two grand noblemen of the court. This is in striking contrast to the end of the story as told by the brothers Grimm. In their version, which was based on German oral tradition, the stepsisters' eyes were pecked out by pigeons, and for their wickedness and falsehood, they were punished with blindness as long as they lived.[14]

Perrault also drew heavily on the Christian concept of morality depicting that the only true gift is grace.

According to Carlson and Decker, the Cinderella view of her dead mother appearing to her aligns suprisingly close to Hinduism and reincarnation.

> Hinduism teaches that based on the law of karma, your good and bad deeds will determine how you will come back in your next life. If you live a bad life and do not do the things required in Hinduism and Buddhism to renounce this world of illusion, you may come back as a lower form.
>
> The first thing that invalidates this [belief] is the fact of the personality of God. The fact that God is personal, that He created us as personal beings, that He has personally revealed Himself to us and that we can have a personal relationship with Him totally does away

with the . . . need for something like re-incarnation.[15]

As for Cinderella's fairy godmother (depicted as a chubby bundle of innocent chuckles à la Clarence, the angel in the Jimmy Stewart film *It's a Wonderful Life*), the roots of her actually being Cinderella's dead mother run deep throughout the entire movie.

Gary Kinnaman, senior pastor of Word of Grace Church in Mesa, Arizona, seems to intimate that the dearly departed fairy godmother may actually be a dark, demonic force. In his book, *Angels Dark and Light*, he writes of the dangers in communicating with the dead:

> As a student of the Bible, I have to believe that reports of the actual souls of the departed revisiting the living probably have their basis in some demonic activity, perhaps a demon in the disguise of a loved one. . . . The Bible, I think, leaves a very slight crack in the door between the living and the dead. In the Gospel accounts, James, Peter and John saw Moses and Elijah, long-departed Old Testament saints, talking with Jesus on the mountain of Christ's transfiguration. The dead, we learn from this, are not really dead. But we also have to notice how Moses and Elijah never said a word to the apostles. In fact, they didn't even

seem to acknowledge their presence. Jesus—not the disembodied spirits of Moses and Elijah—is the center of the account and the focus of everyone's attention. Jesus is the only link between heaven and earth, the ladder upon whom angels ascend and descend (John 1:51). Jesus is our intermediary, not a medium.[16]

Along with Disney's obsession with death came his overwhelming fixation to do everything his way and to make the name Disney recognized worldwide.

In an almost arrogant fashion, Disney adopted, then reworked, some of the most endearing and classical fairy tales of all time. "Grist for a mighty mill," Schickel described it, "in the ineffable Hollywood term." Disney, Schickel said, treated these classics as "properties" to do with as the proprietor of the machine would.[17]

It was long known that Disney was playing fast and loose with the stories of others. But Schickel says the copying was rampant and shameful.

You could throw jarring popular songs into the brew, you could gag them up, you could sentimentalize them. You had, in short, no obligation to the originals or to the cultural tradition they represented. In fact, when it came to billing, J.M. Barrie's *Peter Pan* somehow became Walt Disney's *Peter Pan,* and Lewis Carroll's *Alice [in Wonderland]* became Walt Disney's *Alice.*[18]

It could be argued that this was a true reflection of what happened to the works in the process of getting to the screen, but the egotism that insists on making another man's work your own through wanton tampering and by advertising claim is not an attractive form of egotism, however it is rationalized. And this kind of annexation was to be a constant in the later life of Disney.[19]

If this chapter seems to be a stretch, stay with me. There's more.

Endnotes

1. *Microsoft Cinemania '95* (Redmond, WA: Microsoft, 1995), CD-ROM.

2. *The Servite Prayer Book* (Newbury, Berkshire, Great Britain: Our Lady's Priory, 1951), p. 26.

3. Arthur Babbit, "Fantasia" (subsection "Limited Returns"), *Cinebooks' Motion Picture Guide Review,* Microsoft Cinemania '95 (Redmond, WA: Microsoft, 1995), CD-ROM.

4. Richard Schickel, *The Disney Version* (New York: Simon & Schuster, 1968), pp. 242-243.

5. Ibid.

6. Ibid., p. 146

7. Ibid.

8. Ron Carlson and Ed Decker, *Fast Facts on False Teachings* (Eugene, OR: Harvest House, 1994), p. 246.

9. Ibid., pp. 246-247.

10. Marc Eliot, *Walt Disney: Hollywood's Dark Prince* (New York: Carol Publishing, 1993), pp. 228-229.

11. Ibid.

12. Marshall Cavendish, *Man, Myth and Magic,* Vol. 2 (New York: Marshall Cavendish, 1995), p. 484.

13. Ibid.

14. Ibid.

15. Carlson and Decker, pp. 246-247.

16. Gary Kinnaman, *Angels Dark and Light* (Ann Arbor, MI: Vine Books, 1994), pp. 144-145.

17. Schickel, p. 296.

18. Ibid.

19. Ibid.

What the Bible Says about Witchcraft and Spiritism

Regard not them that have familiar spirits, neither seek after wizards, to be defiled by them: I am the LORD your God. (Leviticus 19:31)

Now the Spirit speaketh expressly, that in the latter times some shall depart from the faith, giving heed to seducing spirits, and doctrines of devils. (1 Timothy 4:1)

Now the works of the flesh are manifest, which are these; adultery, fornication, uncleanness, lasciviousness, idolatry, **witchcraft,** *hatred, variance, emulations, wrath, strife, seditions, heresies, envyings, murders, drunkenness, revellings, and such like: of the which I tell you before, as I have also told you in time past, that they which do such things shall not inherit the kingdom of God. (Galatians 5:19-21,* emphasis added)

Shall a man make gods unto himself, and they are no gods? (Jeremiah 16:20)

Chapter 3

Of Fairies, Witches and Grimm

Fable animals are not real animals. They are human beings in the guise of bird and beast. From his earliest beginnings, as his cave drawings eloquently attest, man has been telling many of his experiences and dramatic conclusions and comments through animal symbols.

—Walt Disney

By the early 1950s Walt Disney had transformed himself from a dreamer of dreams to one of Hollywood's most powerful men. One hit film followed another: *Dumbo, Pinocchio, The Reluctant Dragon, Bambi, Cinderella, Treasure Island, Alice in Wonderland, Robin Hood.* Disney now set his sights on the story of an innocent boy and a little fairy minx who has come to symbolize Disney as much as, if not more than, Mickey Mouse.

Tinker Bell the Bombshell

Disney premiered *Peter Pan* with posters enticing moviegoers to "See the Land Beyond Imagination Where Adventure Never Ends." What he showed them was a romantic, almost attainable Never-Never Land of forests, prairies, lagoons and exquisite color. Kids of all ages were mesmerized as they watched Peter and Wendy soar over the rooftops of Parliament, beneath Tower Bridge, across the river and toward the "second star on the right."

The special effects were dazzling, and Peter Pan's flying sequences were exceptional. But throughout the movie, it wasn't Peter, Wendy, the other children, Captain Hook, Mr. Smee or the tick-tocking alligator who garnered the most attention from the audience. It was Tinker Bell.

In the original play (not created by Disney), Tink, as Pan called her, was shown as just a tiny beam of light. But in the movie, animators had to make her memorable. In Disney's hands she became a curvaceous little blonde bombshell. One member of the movie preview group offered this somewhat startling revelation: "Tinker Bell is just terrible. She should be sweet and dainty, more like the fairies in *Fantasia*. She looks like a nightclub dame."[1]

Other reviewers lambasted the film as a whole. One reviewer implied that Disney was little more than a copycat animator. "Having mutilated 'Alice in Wonderland,' he now murders 'Peter 'an,' and I hate the assumed innocence with which he does it."[2]

Film critic Paul Holt again brought up the sexual implications of Disney's films, a charge that had dogged Walt since *Fantasia*. "In place of childhood dreaming," Holt wrote, "there is strip-cartoon violence and constant hints at sex."[3]

Not just the film critics, but moviegoers as well were picking up on the increasingly overt sexual imagery and energy portrayed in Disney's films. *Peter Pan* was no exception, with Pan's libidinous sidekick Tinker Bell.

But fairies, not unlike Tink, were thought to have existed since ancient times when they were said to have visited and negatively affected newborn babies in their cradles.

As with all mythological suppositions, fairies, and their cousins the pixies, hobs, goblins and gnomes, have their roots in satanic worship and belief in spiritism.

Fairies abound in a perfect world often parallel to the real one. They work, hunt, dance, make music and live in a utopian society totally exempt from death, suffering and change. They call their world the Land of Ever Young, so closely aligned to Peter Pan's Never-Never Land that it defies an opposite conclusion.

And these tiny, flying characters can be, according to legend and primitive religion, helpful, loving, innocent and precious—not unlike Tink—but then can turn on mortal man and strike him with disease or destroy his food supplies at the whims of their own impetuous nature.

Fairies are also thought to be unforgotten gods, the spirits of streams and lakes, and mermaids; spirits of individual trees or of woods, guardians of animals, plants and growing crops.[4]

Certain fairies are called *banshees*. They can attach themselves to an entire family, much as Tinker Bell, with a little prodding from Pan, attached herself to Wendy and company. These banshees are considered ancestral ghosts. Those who fully embrace the lore believe they can hear the banshee sobbing before any member of its special family dies.[5]

The fairy world even has its own take on Moses and the Red Sea. It seems there was a banshee of sorts, sometimes referred to as a *brownie*, who hopped from one family to another, always leaving when practical jokes were played on him. This particular brownie happened by a farm where he struck up a great friendship with a man named Moses, who went to fight for the king but was killed in battle.

The brownie went berserk, according to legend, and became so troublesome that he was hooked by the nose with an awl and pinned down while an exorcism was performed. The brownie was released and a magical wind catapulted him away to the Red Sea, where he performed some equally amazing magic, never quite forgetting his pal Moses.[6]

Because of their sometimes benevolent properties, fairies were and are also thought to be angels doing good deeds for mankind, albeit with a short fuse. If they're pampered they'll work hard, even to the point of cleaning up your home. Their code of morality is also the antithesis of what the Bible teaches. They take anything they want or need, but if a mortal steals from them they rain down a storm of curses.

Fairies seem to promote sexual openness. They have a more than fleeting interest in fertility and are extremely friendly toward lovers. They consider themselves brimming with wisdom, but they are self-indulgent in the extreme. They will steal babies from their cradles, replacing them with animal-like creatures. All the while they masquerade as angelic helpers, do-gooders and beautiful rays of light.[7]

Disney used so many fairy-like creatures in his films, characters that so closely resemble the mystic myth of fairies that the coincidence cannot be ignored or easily explained away. And since fairies also took on the properties and personalities of witches, especially concerning levitation and methods of flight (and Disney films are big on witches), it is conceivable that a more malevolent force was at play in the strategy and concept of his films than even he realized.

Consider, for example, *Peter Pan*. To take flight, all one had to do was hold to Pan or Tink—or be sprinkled by Tink's magic dust. According to ancient fairy lore, fairies use twigs, not broomsticks, and invoke a dark incantation to take flight. There are stories about both witches and fairies who are joined by mortals in magically charmed flight. Frequently they journey to a distant castle or palace where they engage in drunken revelry.[8] So pleasurable were the flights that many humans claimed the fairies were angels on a mission of good. This is affirmed throughout *Peter Pan,* but especially when Tinker Bell helps the children get back home.

Messengers or Menaces?

There is little doubt that the popularity of fairies in Disney films has changed public attitudes about them. To many viewers captivated by Tinker Bell's good deeds, she really did have divine-like properties. Or did she?

In explaining who angels really are and what they do, author Terry Law says that the chief assignment for these beings is not so much to carry messages or help earthlings in trouble as it is to praise and worship God, effectively dispelling several myths not only about angels but also about fairies and witches.

> Michael, the only [angel] specifically called "archangel" in the Bible, apparently has an assignment as a military leader. This probably makes him head of the warrior angels. Michael stands up for God's people and opposes God's

enemies, but always under the authority of God. Gabriel, whom most people believe is an archangel, although he is never called that in the Bible, is God's leading or highest-ranking messenger.

Other angels are also identified by the service they carry out. These are angels of judgment, angels designated as "watchers," angels of the abyss, [the] angel over fire [and the] angel of the waters.[9]

Angels certainly are messengers from God and they do protect and defend us, Law says. But it only happens through God's will. Law goes on to mention what angels cannot do. One major point he brings up is that they do not act on their own. Angels of God (the devil also has angels) neither command nor receive worship.[10]

"Suffice it to pinpoint the relevance of angels by saying that if at any time we stand in need of their ministry, we shall receive it," points out theologian J.I. Packer, "and that as the world watches Christians in hope of seeing them tumble, so do good angels watch Christians in hope of seeing grace triumph in their lives."[11]

The Bible says, "Satan himself is transformed into an angel of light. Therefore it is no great thing if his ministers [*his* angels] also be transformed as the ministers of righteousness" (2 Corinthians 11:14-15). Nor is it a far stretch to assume that impressionable children can be negatively influenced by mythical creatures such as fairies.

But in a study of fairy legends, it is quite startling to discover just how much Disney perceived about their personalities and antics. He seemed aware of how much these fairies align with satanic beliefs.

Anton LaVey, Church of Satan founder, structured the basic teaching of his church in the form of nine satanic statements. He lists them prominently at the front of his *Satanic Bible*. They are virtually an exact skeleton of fairy lore:

1. Satan represents indulgence instead of abstinence.
2. Satan represents vital existence instead of spiritual pipe dreams.
3. Satan represents undefiled wisdom instead of hypocritical self-deceit.
4. Satan represents kindness to those who deserve it instead of love wasted on ingrates.
5. Satan represents vengeance instead of turning the other cheek.
6. Satan represents responsibility to the responsible instead of concern for psychic vampires.
7. Satan represents man as just another animal, sometimes better, more often worse than those that walk on all fours, who because of his "divine, spiritual and intellectual development" has become the most vicious animal of all.

8. Satan represents all of the so-called sins, as they all lead to physical or mental gratification.
9. Satan has been the best friend the church has ever had, as he has kept it in business all these years.[12]

Says Packer,

> Acknowledging Satan's reality, taking his opposition seriously, noting his strategy (anything, provided it be not biblical Christianity), and reckoning on always being at war with him—this is not a lapse into a dualistic concept of two gods, one good, one evil, fighting it out. Satan is a creature, superhuman but not divine. He has much knowledge and power, but he is neither omniscient nor omnipotent; he can move around in ways humans cannot, but he is not omnipresent; and he is an already defeated rebel, having no more power than God allows him and being destined for the lake of fire.[13]

Flirting with the Dark Side

In 1956, Disney once again proved that he could promote Satanism, witchcraft and demonic mythology as well as anyone, with another of his fairy tale adaptations—*Sleeping Beauty*, a reluctant heroine who lies in enchanted sleep for a century until her prince arrives and revives her with a kiss.

Almost a complete flop at the box office, the film grossed only a little over $5 million, even though it promoted the obligatory fairies—Flora, Fauna and Merryweather—and had an abundance of cute little animals, sans any personality.

Clearly adapted from the tales of Charles Perrault's classic *La Belle au Bois Dormant*, there was only one notable character in the entire animated film, according to critics—the ultra-evil, jealous queen Maleficent, who turns herself into a dragon and does battle with Prince Phillip.

For the most part, audiences didn't know that Sleeping Beauty's predicament was grounded in a centuries-old European black magic charm. It was called the hand of glory. It was the hand cut from the body of a man who had been hanged. After it was dried and pickled, it was used as a holder for a candle made from the man's fat. When this charm was brought into a house and lit, everyone inside would supposedly fall into a deep sleep.[14]

There were variations on the theme. The Southern Slavs used a human bone thrown over the house to induce sleep on those inside. In Java, ne'er-do-wells threw dirt from a grave into the house. Hindus placed human ashes in front of the door. Peruvians used other assorted body parts, all of them burned. In Mexico it was the left arm of a woman who had died in childbirth.

These magical formulas to induce sleep were usually employed by those wishing to burglarize the house in question. All came with a variety of prayers, rhymes and prose. All were based on the satanic desecration of graves or corpses.

A magically induced sleep or trance can be a by-product of voodoo, an offshoot of black magic focusing on a distant god who manifests himself through various rituals.

Maleficent's depiction in *Sleeping Beauty*, her potions, her egomania, her obsessions are all traits of witches. And when she changes herself into a dragon, she's in true form.

In black magic and witchcraft, there is a persistent idea that witches can turn themselves at will into animals. Such beliefs, particularly those in which the witch takes on an animal shape to perform some evil deed, have been confused with the keeping of a familiar spirit. But there is a distinction. The true familiar spirit, according to Cavendish, is a demon kept by the witch and totally distinct from herself.[15]

Bob Larson, an expert on witchcraft and Satanism but also a Christian, says that all forms of witchcraft are contrary to Scripture. They must be avoided at all cost.

> Witchcraft denies biblical doctrines of heaven and hell, original sin and the denunciation of demons. Scripture repeatedly denounces witchcraft. The elemental forces conjured are demons, and

the horned deity revered is the devil. Though white witches claim to be benevolent, all such association with the spirit world is forbidden by the Bible.[16]

Frightening Figures

Many adults are quick to protest any censure of Disney for the mythology, witchcraft, sorcery and black magic in his films. They themselves have had a steady diet of Disney since they were kids and they grew up just fine.

But some haven't been as fortunate.

Two of the Disney animators, Frank Thomas and Ollie Johnston, both well-known, say there's an important issue here. "[The Disney malefactors] may be too frightening for the audience," they say, "especially children."[17]

Thomas and Johnston go on to say:

> We want the viewers to believe and be emotionally moved by the conflict they are watching. But there is no advantage in crossing the line into something that is too scary for comfort.
>
> [Children] like to be thrilled, but not terrified. Reactions, of course, vary widely depending on the age and maturity of individuals and the experiences they have had in their lives.[18]

The two animators, both of whom worked directly with Walt Disney, point out that some children are unduly influenced. A Disney film can scar them for life.

> One youngster will hide his eyes. Another will turn his back to the screen and deliberately look at other objects in the theater. Others will watch, bug-eyed, as if hypnotized, no matter how dramatic the situation becomes. Some will have nightmares for weeks, even years, and possibly will never want to see the picture again. . . . Then there is a smaller group that become so involved with the characters that they feel they are actually in the story themselves.[19]

Packer points out that the nurture of our children is paramount if we are going to raise them biblically. That responsibility falls upon the entire family structure. "Children must be instructed and must be encouraged to take instruction seriously as a basis for their living," he says. "Discipline, which means directive and corrective training, is necessary to lead children beyond childish folly to self-controlled wisdom."[20]

Part of that guidance could involve guiding children away from, not into, a Disney film—especially if the film can only promise fear, nightmares and the potential of occult influence for the rest of their lives.

Both Thomas and Johnston, in describing their impetus in doing their book on villains, seem to quote and adhere to the philosophy of a *Los Angeles Times* reporter who wrote a 1992 article about evil in our lives. "We need terror by which to measure and enjoy our comfort," the article boasted. "We need thrills to ameliorate the tedium. We need evil to locate our good. And evil is a concept that has been increasingly undervalued and ignored."[21]

Endnotes

1. Richard Holliss and Brian Sibley, *The Disney Studio Story* (New York: Crown Books, 1988), p. 64.

2. Ibid.

3. Ibid.

4. Marshall Cavendish, *Man, Myth and Magic*, Vol. 4 (New York: Marshall Cavendish, 1995), p. 901.

5. Ibid.

6. Ibid.

7. Ibid.

8. Ibid., p. 902.

9. Terry Law, *The Truth about Angels* (Orlando, FL: Creation House, 1994), pp. 117-121.

10. Ibid.

11. J.I. Packer, *A Concise Theology* (Wheaton, IL: Tyndale House, 1993), p. 65.

12. J. Gordon Melton, "Religious Creeds," *The Encyclopedia of American Religion* (Detroit, MI: Gale Research, 1988), p. 765.

13. Packer, p. 70.

14. Cavendish, p. 2401.

15. Ibid., Vol. 4, p. 914.

16. Bob Larson, *Larson's New Book of Cults* (Wheaton, IL: Tyndale House, 1982), p. 467.

17. Ollie Johnston and Frank Thomas, *The Disney Villain* (New York: Hyperion, 1993), p. 27.

18. Ibid.

19. Ibid.

20. Packer, p. 233.

21. Johnston and Thomas, preface.

What the Bible Says
about Evil

This know also, that in the last days perilous times shall come. For men shall be lovers of their own selves, covetous, boasters, proud, blasphemers, disobedient to parents, unthankful, unholy, without natural affection, trucebreakers, false accusers, incontinent, fierce, despisers of those that are good, traitors, heady, highminded, lovers of pleasures more than lovers of God; having a form of godliness, but denying the power thereof: from such turn away. (2 Timothy 3:1-5)

Your glorying is not good. Know ye not that a little leaven leaveneth the whole lump? Purge out therefore the old leaven, that ye may be a new lump, as ye are unleavened. (1 Corinthians 5:6-7)

Let not sin therefore reign in your mortal body, that ye should obey it in the lusts thereof. Neither yield ye your members as instruments of unrighteousness unto sin. (Romans 6:12-13)

Now the works of the flesh are manifest, which are these; adultery, fornication, uncleanness, lasciviousness, idolatry, witchcraft, hatred, variance, emulations, wrath, strife, seditions, heresies, envyings, murders, drunkenness, revellings, and such like: of the which I tell you before, as I have also told you in time past, that they which do such things shall not inherit the kingdom of God. (Galatians 5:19-21)

For the love of money is the root of all evil. (1 Timothy 6:10)

What man is he that desireth life, and loveth many days, that he may see good? Keep thy tongue from evil, and thy lips from speaking guile. Depart from evil, and do good; seek peace, and pursue it. (Psalm 34:12-14)

Ah sinful nation, a people laden with iniquity, a seed of evildoers, children that are corrupters: they have forsaken the LORD, they have provoked the Holy One of Israel unto anger, they are gone away backward. (Isaiah 1:4)

Woe to the rebellious children, saith the LORD, that take counsel, but not of me; and that cover with a covering, but not of my spirit, that they may add sin to sin. (Isaiah 30:1)

Chapter 4

The Rebirth of Disney

I feel every person creates his own determinism by discovering his best aptitudes and following them undeviatingly.

—*Walt Disney*

Well into the 1950s and the early 1960s Disney's organization grew and prospered. It produced some fairly good movies: *20,000 Leagues Under the Sea, Old Yeller, Kidnapped* and *Swiss Family Robinson.* The premiere of the blockbuster television series, "Walt Disney Presents," brought such legends as "Davy Crockett" and "Zorro" into the homes of North America's families. Disneyland in southern California capped off an era unequaled in Hollywood entertainment.

To be sure, there were a few box office flops, *Fantasia* the most notable, though it later made money for the organization through re-releases.

On the whole, however, Walt Disney's reputation was unfettered. He was thought of as a gen-
ius moviemaker in charge of a multimillion
dollar corporate fortress.

But eventually the reigning king of animation
had to face his mortality. Walt's left lung, riddled
with tumors the size of walnuts, had to be removed, and the surgery proved too much for his
weakened body. On December 15, 1966, Walt
Disney died of circulatory system failure at St
Joseph's Hospital, across from his Burbank Studios.[1]

During his lifetime, Walt Disney received
more than 700 honors. They included twenty-
nine Oscars, four Emmys, the Irving Thalberg
Award, the Presidential Freedom Medal and the
French Legion of Honor. All of them were in
recognition of his outstanding contribution to
the world of film.[2]

Unexpected Condolences

At Disney's death, one condolence telegram
directed to Walt's widow, Lillian, came from an
unexpected source:

> INDEED SORRY TO LEARN OF PASSING OF YOUR
> HUSBAND AND WANT TO EXTEND MY HEARTFELT
> SYMPATHY. I KNOW WORDS ARE MOST INADE-
> QUATE TO EASE YOUR GRIEF, BUT IT IS MY HOPE
> THAT YOU WILL DERIVE CONSOLATION FROM
> KNOWING THAT HIS OUTSTANDING CONTRIBU-

TIONS WILL BE A LASTING MEMORIAL TO HIM.
HIS DEDICATION TO THE HIGHEST STANDARDS
OF MORAL VALUES AND HIS ACHIEVEMENTS WILL
ALWAYS STAND AS AN INSPIRATION TO THOSE
WHO WERE PRIVILEGED TO KNOW HIM.

JOHN EDGAR HOOVER [3]

The head of the Federal Bureau of Investigation a Disney fan? To be sure. But Hoover was more. He was reportedly Disney's boss. Disney had been among the earliest and most forceful of the film community's anti-communists. From October, 1940, he had been a loyal and dedicated domestic spy for the FBI. His assignment: Report anything that might be of interest to the Bureau.[4]

Disney allegedly filed dozens of reports on what he believed to be subversive communist activities. They included a fund-raiser for the Council for Pan-American Democracy, a Latin American civil rights organization thought to be communist. Disney also filed reports on actors, directors and screenwriters who evidenced communist activity or sympathy. Many of them would eventually be subpoenaed by the House Un-American Activities Committee. Later Disney's name became linked to the infamous "Hollywood blacklist" of movie professionals whose lives were virtually destroyed by the roster.[5]

When Walt Disney died, much of the world mourned the loss of its "Uncle Walt." They saw in his death the passing of the age of innocence. But others would recall a very different Disney legacy, one of shattered careers and ruined lives.

Many rank-and-file employees could not forget his radical, right-wing anti-unionism. Others remembered his key role in bringing the House Un-American Activities Committee crashing down on Hollywood's elite.[6]

A Studio without Direction

There was something else that seemed to come crashing down with Disney's death: the entirety of the Disney organization. Disney, as many would learn, was irreplaceable. His death caused a fierce internal crisis within the corporation.

For years the Disney organization had been split into two factions. One adhered to Walt's principles of creativity. The other championed brother Roy's practical side. Walt was the only person with the force and ingenuity to keep this delicate coalition together. Now the "magnet" was gone.

Disney executives and presidents came and went. Wall Street gurus viewed Disney Studios as ripe for the plucking. There were rumors of both friendly and hostile takeovers.

Disney stock declined. By the mid-1980s, it had dropped from $84 a share to $45. The studio was assailed by high stakes investors seeking big profits. Among the heavy hitters swarming in and out of the Disney organization were junk bond king Michael Milken. The notorious wheeler-dealer, Ivan Boesky, became the fourth largest stockholder in the studio.

Meanwhile, Disney Studios was still cranking out movies. They restructured a new adult-oriented production company, Walt Disney Pictures, in hopes of capturing a more diverse market.

One of the company's first attempts was a picture entitled *Country*, starring Jessica Lange. The film, which some critics dubbed the feminist version of *Grapes of Wrath*, was a box office catastrophe.

Next on the menu was *Trenchcoat*, a comedy-drama starring Margot Kidder and Robert Hays. The two were entangled in international intrigue and undercover spy shenanigans à la the highly successful TV series, "The Scarecrow and Mrs. King." *Trenchcoat*, however, was scarcely more successful than *Country*.

An Ominous Turn

Disney's next effort was ominous and, by virtue of its title alone, some say it prophesied not only what the movie was about, but also what the Disney organization was embracing. Based on the Ray Bradbury thriller, *Something Wicked This Way Comes* was heavy, relentless horror.

Set in the early 1900s, the story was about a carnival that came to a small, family-oriented American town. Mr. Dark, the carnival owner (played by Jonathan Pryce), could have been Satan incarnate.

He promised to fulfill everyone's dreams, albeit for a heavy, evil price. He delivered, but what Mr Dark did to that innocent, God-fearing town was reminiscent of Satan's ages-long scheme. Author Robert Morey, executive director of the Research and Educational Foundation, says that Satan's devices are many.

Satan is able to motivate people to do things by putting ideas in their minds. He put it into the mind of [King] David to number the people [of Israel] (1 Chronicles 21:1).

Satan can implant thoughts even in believers. David was not a pagan. Yet Satan was able to manipulate him into doing something that would harm both him and the nation. Satan can take something which seems perfectly innocent and use it to do evil. Taking a census of men of fighting age is hardly wrong in and of itself. In the book of Numbers, God Himself commanded such a census be taken. Why then was it viewed as sin [in David's time]? When David told Joab to number the people, Joab sensed that this was not the right thing to do at the time. There was no war. There was no need to enlarge the army. Besides, God had not commanded it.[7]

What about Mr. Dark's fulfillment of everyone's dreams? Morey goes on to say that Satan can and does imitate miracles.

> Satan loves to duplicate the miracles that God does, even if he has to cheat to do it. This is why he is said to do "counterfeit miracles, signs and wonders" (2 Thessalonians 2:9, NIV). These counterfeit miracles may at times be so clever and deceptive that no one can discover how the fraud is done, but it is a fraud nonetheless.[8]

More Movie Mortalities

Something Wicked would not be Disney Studios' last box office fizzle. To make matters worse, the organization had to endure a second major movie mortality. *Tron* was the story of humans being absorbed body and soul by computers. No one seemed to care.

The failures continued to mount. *Never Cry Wolf* prompted one reviewer to comment that the only hand Disney had in it was the one signing the check to pay for it.[9]

But, tragically, there was more. Disney's $40-million erratum, *The Black Cauldron*, was a studio return to animation sans any of Disney's original animators (except for Eric Larson, who remained only in a consulting position). The film was a sword-and-sorcery tale of a boy who had to find a powerful black cauldron before it fell into the hands of the baneful Horned King and his army of skeletal Deathless Warriors. It didn't make a big enough spatter at the box office to tempt Disney execs to throw their hearts and souls into more animation, and was so disappointing that company morale plummeted.

The exaltation of sorcery and black magic in this film, though, is virtually gratuitous. For example, in one scene, the Horned King leads his army in a vicious attack, lifting skeletal remains high above his head, and unduly emphasizes cruel horror and despair. In a capsulated form, *The Black Cauldron* is a melting pot of voodoo, black magic, Satanism, witchcraft and just enough *Santeria*[10] thrown in to glorify the gods and goddesses of the occult.

Roy Disney's assessment of the picture was a bit surprising. Even though the Horned King was as powerfully evil as any Disney creation had ever been, Roy felt the character didn't go far enough. In Roy's opinion, the use of close-ups and too much activity gave the impression of a man who could be argued with. Roy thought he should have been as unreachable and intimidating as Chernobog. No one should speak in his presence. The words should wither in one's throat. Viewers should not even know if this evil creature was man, animal or demon. The Horned King was unlimited power on the verge of taking over the world and somehow he had to be stopped. Such was the special challenge Roy saw for the tiny band of characters who carried the hope of the future on their uncertain shoulders.[11]

Another film that bears closer scrutiny is a little-known Disney adventure called *The Journey of Natty Gann*, about a girl who travels across the country during the Depression in order to be reunited with her father. Along the way she strikes up a relationship with a wolf, who acts as her friend, guide, protector and guardian.

Ironically, in the occult, wolves are thought to be benevolent creatures created by evil spirits. Friendly wolves are most common in mythical tradition and have even been known to pray for their benefactors to their own deities. Wolves have even been depicted as rearers of children, as in another Disney production—*The Jungle Book*, created originally by Rudyard Kipling.

According to Greek mythology, gods and goddesses frequently took on the forms of wolves, but over and above that, the wolf has innumerable associations with the devil.[12]

The devil sometimes took a wolf's shape, and wolves have been proven to have ancient relationship with witchcraft. Witches are said to howl like wolves and use portions of the animal in their charms. And in witchcraft's *Beast Fable*, a crafty wolf sings Psalm 23.[13]

To be sure, it is not a far stretch from the guardianship of Natty Gann's wolf, with all of its positive, paladin properties, to mythological and even occultic symbolism.

Enter Michael Eisner

Somewhere amid the chaos, fiascoes and inadequacies, and after the smoke cleared and the critics fell silent for a short time, Michael Eisner walked through the doors of Disney. He came at the behest of then Disney head, Ron Miller, whom Disney's widow believed had mismanaged the studio to such an extent that it was in jeopardy of being destroyed.[14]

On September 22, 1984, Eisner—the former president of Paramount Pictures, with credits like *Saturday Night Fever*, *Grease*, *An Officer and a Gentleman*, *Terms of Endearment* and *Raiders of the Lost Ark* under his belt—was appointed to head Walt Disney Productions. Along with partner Frank Wells, Eisner brought Jeffrey Katzenberg over from his home at Paramount Pictures.

Together, the team completely revamped the entire Disney operation, shedding a lot of employee dead weight. Most of the Disney administrative staff were asked to resign and many others were terminated on the spot.

After the first year, around 400 employees were terminated by Eisner and replaced by hand-picked, ultra-loyal colleagues previously at Paramount. Disney's organization had finally been successfully stormed and conquered by the dominant Hollywood aristocracy.

One of the most significant changes Eisner would make was the addition of David Hoberman, who was put in charge of a new Disney arm called Touchstone Pictures.

By then, Walt Disney Productions was on the brink of financial insolvency. Disney needed a hit picture worse than a compulsive gambler needs the next roll of the dice. The hit came with a movie called *Splash*. Because of the film's sexual overtones and high-level carnality, Eisner made sure it was under the Touchstone label. He knew such a picture would tarnish the perceived public image of Walt Disney Productions.

Splash, the story of a mermaid (Daryl Hannah) who falls in love with a man (Tom Hanks) created a unique sexual magic and movie-long erotic tension that critics loved.

Noted film historian Pauline Kael, for example, described Hannah as having long blond tresses, wide blue eyes, smiling curvy lips and the look of a beautifully sexy Nordic goddess.[15]

It was clear. *Splash* would be Disney's libidinous coming-out party, and it was a tremendous success, with hardly anyone not connected with Hollywood knowing that under the guise of Touchstone, *Splash* was a Disney picture.

Attack on the Family

So blatant were the sexual images and messages in *Splash* that a lengthy dissertation on the evils of premarital sex is not warranted. Author Robert Morey, however, notes that a powerful satanic device that has been quite effective in destroying the American family is the infiltration of wicked words, deeds, attitudes and clothing.[16] In his book *Satan's Devices*, Morey goes on to say,

> When parents allow evil to flourish in the home, it creates an ungodly atmosphere which smothers a child's thirst for the things of God and encourages a thirst for the things of this world instead.[17]

Morey also says that Satan uses many other devices in putting the family under siege, including pornography, fornication, adultery and sodomy. If we don't raise our children to respect the Lord, he says, we'll end up with wicked children as Eli did in First Samuel 2:12.

Under Eisner and Katzenberg's watchful, meticulous eye, Disney Corporation, alias Touchstone Pictures, became the shining star of the American film industry, producing adult-oriented movies that scored big at the box office. Disney's Touchstone label began to post greater profits than at any other time in the corporation's history.[18]

But Eisner wasn't finished. He brought over another Paramount wizard, Richard Frank, to help Disney's directionless television interests. Years before Walt had organized Buena Vista Distribution to handle the TV marketplace but, reportedly, it had gone soft. Frank's role would be to do for Disney television what Touchstone was doing for Disney motion pictures.

With a strong track record at Paramount—
Frank was responsible for such mega-hits as "Entertainment Tonight" and "Solid Gold"—he was
to be Disney's "other" golden boy, developing
one of the most successful television sitcoms of
the eighties, "Golden Girls."

The story of three aging bachelorettes and an
ill-tempered but lovable old woman took the nation by storm. Their antics, dating habits and
tensions with ex-husbands were considered cute
and innocent, but were they?

The on-air overt sexual enthusiasm of one of
the stars, Rue McClanahan, was shown with almost adolescent guilelessness. She pursued conquest after conquest, with North America's
living rooms her unwitting accomplices.

The show assaulted traditional family values.
In one episode, for example, Blanche's daughter
used artificial insemination to conceive a child,
winning her mother's support.[19]

Religion also took a mugging from the sitcom.
In another episode, an adopted woman discovers
that her natural father was a corrupt, less-than-
pious monk who had had a torrid affair with the
monastery cook.[20]

Financial Success, But at What Price?

Not everyone was pleased with the direction
Eisner was taking Disney, however—not the
least of which was noted author Leonard Mosley.
In his striking biographical look at Disney, *Dis-*

ney's World, he encapsulates the impact of Eisner on "The House That Walt Built."

> All [Walt's] talented artists are either dead or have disappeared into the obscurity of old age. Even Mickey Mouse and Donald Duck are animated nowadays on computers.
>
> The studio has abandoned Davy Crockett, flying autos, magic rubber and absent-minded professors in favor of "adult" films featuring braless [sic] mermaids. The studio is now so "adult" that at any moment they are likely to show a computer-animated Pluto having intercourse with one of the 101 Dalmatians.
>
> The toughest moneymen in Hollywood have taken over the lot on Buena Vista, and the whole nature of the studio's business is changing.[21]

Endnotes

1. Marc Eliot, *Walt Disney: Hollywood's Dark Prince* (New York: Carol Publishing, 1993), p. 265.
2. Ibid.
3. Ibid., p. 168.
4. Ibid., p. 169.
5. Ibid., pp. 169-185.
6. Ibid., p. 265.

7. Robert Morey, *Satan's Devices* (Eugene, OR: Harvest House, 1993), pp. 50-51.

8. Ibid., pp. 72-73.

9. Richard Holliss and Brian Sibley, *The Disney Studio Story* (New York: Crown Books, 1988), p. 104.

10. Melton, J. Gordon, "Voodoo," *Encyclopedia of American Religions* (Detroit, MI: Gale Research, 1993), sec. 1362, pp. 852-853. According to Melton, *Santeria* is an Afro-Cuban voodoo religion derived from the Yoruba religion, which many consider to be the rain forest version of the Ancient Egyptian Mystery System.

11. Ollie Johnston and Frank Thomas, *The Disney Villain* (New York: Hyperion, 1984), p. 170.

12. Marshall Cavendish, *Man, Myth and Magic*, Vol. 11 (New York: Marshall Cavendish, 1995), p. 3049.

13. Ibid.

14. Holliss and Sibley, p. 276.

15. Pauline Kael, *Cinemania* (Redmond, WA: Microsoft, 1995).

16. Morey, p. 152.

17. Ibid.

18. *Cinemania: Baseline's Encyclopedia of Film* (Redmond, WA: Microsoft, 1995), CD-ROM.

19. Michael Medved, *Hollywood vs. America* (New York: Harper Perennial, 1992), p. 143.

20. Ibid., p. 81.

21. Leonard Mosely, *Disney's World* (New York: Stein & Day, 1985), p. 307.

What the Bible Says about Example and Influence

Then said he unto the disciples, It is impossible but that offences will come: but woe unto him, through whom they come! It were better for him that a millstone were hanged about his neck, and he cast into the sea, than that he should offend one of these little ones. (Luke 17:1-2)

Let no man despise thy youth; but be thou an example of the believers, in word, in conversation, in charity, in spirit, in faith, in purity. (1 Timothy 4:12)

Thou shalt make no covenant with [the Canaanites], nor with their gods. They shall not dwell in thy land, lest they make thee sin against me: for if thou serve their gods, it will surely be a snare unto thee. (Exodus 23:32-33)

What the Bible Says about Marriage and Adultery

And [Jesus] answered and said unto them, Have ye not read, that he which made them at the beginning made them male and female, and said, For this cause shall a man leave father and mother, and shall cleave to his wife: and they twain shall be one flesh? Wherefore they are no more twain, but one flesh. What therefore God hath joined together, let not man put asunder. (Matthew 19:4-6)

Thou shalt not commit adultery. (Exodus 20:14)

Thou shalt not covet thy neighbour's wife. (Exodus 20:17)

And the man that committeth adultery with another man's wife . . . the adulterer and the adulteress shall surely be put to death. (Leviticus 20:10)

If a man be found lying with a woman married to an husband, then they shall both of them die, both the man that lay with the woman, and the woman: so shalt thou put away evil from Israel. (Deuteronomy 22:22)

But I [Jesus] say unto you, that whosoever looketh on a woman to lust after her hath committed adultery with her already in his heart. (Matthew 5:28)

Chapter 5

"Honey, I Copied the Kids"

*Money is something I understand only
vaguely and think about only when I don't
have enough to finance my current enthusiasm, whatever it may be. All I know about
money is that I have to have it to do things.*

—Walt Disney

Many Hollywood old-timers speculate that
Walt Disney made movies which mirrored
and caricatured himself—his flaws, his yearnings
and the life he never had.

If that was so, and from all indications it was,
it could be held that the current Disney film
genre paints an outrageous portrait of all that is
Hollywood and all that has become the once-
lauded studio of the "Mouse That Roared."

And if one were to pick a movie that encom-
passes all of the degenerative properties, the outlandish excesses, the perverted psyche and the

extreme despair of Glitterville, it would have to be the 1986 Disney comedy, *Down and Out in Beverly Hills*.

Taken from the obscure yet critically accepted 1932 French film *Boudu Saved from Drowning* (directed by Jean Renoir), *Down and Out* was revamped, repackaged, rewritten, recast, respiced and reissued as only Disney could do with impunity. This Paul Mazursky film was little more than 103 minutes of sheer sex, degeneration, unrequited overindulgence and a wanton lewdness that might have made Sodom pale by comparison.

As the storyline goes, a bum (Nick Nolte) wanders into the backyard of a Beverly Hills family (Richard Dreyfuss, Bette Midler and Tracy Nelson) and tries to kill himself in their swimming pool. After he is saved, the family takes him in and he proceeds to live off of them while playing musical beds with the wife (whose life involves long sessions with young, masculine masseurs, Eastern yogis and psychotherapists), the daughter and the maid (who is also sleeping with the husband). Perhaps the only morally bright light in the entire picture may be that Nolte's wandering libido didn't go after the family's sexually confused, androgynous son.

Not All the Critics Liked the Film

Down and Out left some of the critics down and out. This was especially so of some who recognized the film's glorification of immoderation and insatiable sex. One critic had this to say:

> After establishing, with all too much conviction, the monstrously foolish nature of its conspicuously consuming characters, as well as the utterly fatuous lives they lead, Mr. Mazursky draws back, as if afraid to acknowledge the truth of his own observations.[1]

Nevertheless, *Down and Out* generated more revenue than Disney had seen in years—over $60 million.[2]

Why is Hollywood so focused on values that supposedly appeal to the lowest common denominator of human nature and subsequently embrace a demonstrated antibiblical posture? According to Michael Medved, Hollywood as a whole has clearly demonstrated an uncompromising contempt for conventional family values.

> The music industry shamelessly promotes promiscuity, motion pictures focus relentlessly on family dysfunction and divorce, while television programs broadcast the deadly message that kids know better than their doltish and irrelevant parents. In other words, the contrast between private contentment and public pessimism that shows up in major polls mirrors the huge chasm be-

tween our own view of the world and Hollywood's—between the relatively happy real-life experience of most American families and the grim and poisonous visions that regularly emerge from the entertainment industry. Those antifamily images have become so deeply ingrained in our national consciousness that few Americans can summon the courage or the strength to dismiss them as the destructive distortions that they are.[3]

A Pledge Betrayed

Family Research Council's Robert Knight seems quite in agreement. He paints a picture of the Disney studio that was and what Disney has become under the ultimate Hollywood authority figure, Michael Eisner:

> When Disney [Pictures] changed hands from essentially family ownership to an insider group of Hollywood executives who already had long track records, the whole tenor of the studio changed and it became strictly a money-making enterprise.
> Even though Michael Eisner had pledged at the outset that Disney would keep its standards, they quickly began bringing Disney into the modern world

by liberal standards—in other words, having Disney reflect the mores of the day rather than a timeless set of values.[4]

Knight says that before Eisner, Disney was a separate and total entity within Hollywood—an oasis in a subculture of liberalism in the purest sense of the word; after Eisner stepped in, the old Disney was swallowed up.

> They started merchandising the Disney library like never before. Films that had been held back for distribution every few years, like *Fantasia,* found their way to video shelves rather quickly. And with this newly amassed capital, the [new] Disney people set out to make the type of movies that everyone else in Hollywood was making.[5]

Knight seems aware of Disney's earlier dalliance with occultism and spiritism and goes on to comment that the Walt Disney Corporation has now become a part of the overall Hollywood fixation on evil too often, too heavily, too much:

> Even if evil loses out in the end, it's the sheer volume that numbs you to it eventually. Instead of evil becoming a counterpoint, it has become the whole point.

Eisner has never said, "Look, we got Disney and we're gonna use the kid empire just so we can make adult films." To give Eisner credit, I think he has a grander vision than that. He sees the whole kid empire as the core of Disney, but as a Hollywood adult-film maker he's entitled to make whatever he wants.[6]

What Eisner Wanted

One of the films Eisner obviously wanted to make was the 1987 gargantuan hit, *Ruthless People*. It centered around a rich and extremely unpleasant man (Danny deVito), complete with two-timing mistress. The man plans to kill his wife (Bette Midler). But when she is kidnapped, he feels the gods have smiled down on him, and he simply refuses to pay the demanded ransom. Instead, he taunts the kidnappers to kill her.

This film, packed with sexual innuendo, adultery, violence and spousal abuse, garnered $70 million.

Very quickly Eisner was earning a track record for pushing out moneymaking films. By early 1987, Disney films had grossed an astounding $511 million.[7]

Not all are favorably impressed by figures like that. Many church leaders regard the new Disney as an unabashed peddler of immorality and licentiousness. Robert Knight believes the moral crisis North America faces today is partly due to what Hollywood does for a living. "I wonder when families are going to wake up and understand that the dollars they're plunking down for Disney movies and products and at theme parks are being used to buy studios that turn out immoral, anti-Christian, pornographic movies."[8]

Billy Graham, in his book, *Storm Warnings*, says we need to heed the winds of change.

> Truly the world is in need of moral leadership. We need moral leadership that teaches the difference between right and wrong and teaches us to forgive one another even as we are forgiven by our Father in heaven.
>
> We need moral leadership that teaches love for our brothers and sisters of every race and tribe; a morality in which material abundance is never the aim or goal of a society, but merely the result of its industry.
>
> We need a morality that guarantees respect for mothers who mother, for fathers who father and for all those who live and work together to fulfill God's commandments to pursue our individual destinies as His privileged children.[9]

A Whole New Standard of Sexual Ethics

The Disney corporation's formidable Hollywood elite has helped to bring a whole new standard of sexual ethics to the forefront of our culture. On one hand, the Disney corporation is concerned about children and wholesome children's programming. On the other hand, the revenues garnered from this enterprise fuel a film genre that is mentally, physically, emotionally and spiritually deadly to those same children.

James Dobson, noted psychologist, author and crusader for family values, warns us as to what it will be like without strong moral fiber:

> Robbed of [moral] sexual standards, society will unravel like a ball of twine. That is the lesson of history. That is the legacy of Rome and more than 2,000 civilizations that have come and gone on this earth. The family is the basic unit of society on which all human activity rests. If you tamper with the sexual nature of familial relationships, you necessarily threaten the entire superstructure. Indeed, ours is swaying like a drunken sailor from the folly of our cultural engineers.[10]

Another extremely popular Disney movie under the Touchstone banner was the typically Rrated drama *The Color of Money*, starring Paul Newman, Tom Cruise and Mary Elizabeth Mastrantonio. The film's storyline, though timeworn and typical, revolves around Newman's character in the 1961 film, *The Hustler*, about a pool shark and his travels through dishonest waters. Newman plays a silver-haired retired pool hustler turned Chicago liquor salesman who discovers a new protégé and takes him under his wing.

The main reason the movie was a hit, besides Paul Newman, was its direction under the leadership of Hollywood's legendary movie mogul director, Martin Scorsese. Scorsese is best remembered, perhaps, not for his helmsmanship in *Raging Bull*, *The Last Waltz* or *Taxi Driver*, but for his impudent and ill-bred depiction of Jesus in the 1988 film, *The Last Temptation of Christ*.

Scorsese's portrayal of Christ as a sexual pervert with leanings toward men as well as women totally enraged the public. When the film opened, more than 25,000 people gathered outside Universal Studios in protest.

"Sour, Fun-Loathing People"

The movie moguls, together with many of their supporters in the news media, persisted in dismissing the demonstrators as a lunatic fringe of religious fanatics and right wing extremists.[11] The protesters were lambasted as "sour, fun-loathing people—the American ignoramus fac-

tion that is perpetually geeked up on self-right-
eous bile."[12]

A vice president of the former Walt Disney
Studios, Ken Wales, was one of the speakers at
the Universal protest. He said in part:

> As a member of this industry, I wish
> that there were hundreds of stars and
> writers and directors standing here
> with me. I suppose they are out protest-
> ing toxic waste. Let me tell you, there is
> toxic waste in other areas besides our
> rivers. That happens in the pollution of
> our minds, our souls and our spirits.[13]

Another author says the signs are there. "To
depict Christ in such a way is telltale," he says of
not only *The Last Temptation*, but of Hollywood's
hostility to Christianity overall. "This is the kind
of stuff that the cults would applaud. The occult
world and New Agers are also likely to favor the
desecration of Jesus because to them, the Son of
God poses a very real threat called exposure."[14]

And of the one-sided, highly prejudicial media
coverage of the protest of *The Last Temptation*,
Medved puts it all into perspective.

> This sort of one-sided coverage made
> it easier for everyone in the industry to
> ignore the uncomfortable questions
> raised by the controversy—questions
> about Hollywood's underlying hostility

to religious belief and to religious believers.

Instead of confronting the situation honestly, show business leaders issued an endless series of smug pronouncements in defense of Mr. Scorsese's First Amendment rights, inconsistently coupled with condemnation of those who chose to exercise their First Amendment rights by protesting the film.[15]

There's a saying, "Hollywood is known by the company it keeps." That Eisner would recruit Scorsese to direct *The Color of Money* may say something about Eisner.

The Disney studio and its alter ego Touchstone were on an expensive roll. With the premiere of *Three Men and a Baby* and other top grossers like *Good Morning Vietnam*, the studio thrived.

But it also had its setbacks. Raunchy, streetwise and ill-bred comedies like *Off Beat*, *Tough Guys*, *Tin Men* and *Ernest Goes to Camp* were disappointing but overshadowed by the big ones.

Roger and Jessica Rabbit

Another of the "big ones" was *Who Framed Roger Rabbit?* Combining live action and animation, it featured almost every Disney cartoon character ever to appear on screen.

Many observed that Roger Rabbit bore a more-than-coincidental likeness to Walt Disney's much earlier Oswald Rabbit that Walt had lost the rights to. But Roger's agenda certainly went far beyond good clean cartoon fun for kids of all ages. In *Roger Rabbit* there was some fairly intense violence as well as outlandish sex dished out by the film's animated femme fatale, Jessica Rabbit.

The story centers around Roger, a cartoon star, who seems to have trouble concentrating due to marital troubles. The owner of the cartoon studio hires a human detective to "get the goods" on Roger's wife, Jessica, who is suspected of having an affair.

Described by critics as being voluptuous, super-sexy and incredibly human-looking, Jessica seems to be a cross between the sensuality of Marilyn Monroe and the vampishness of Madonna, complete with over-developed breasts and a long, clingy dress with a slit up the side almost to the waist.

In one bar scene, Jessica Rabbit, who sings a seductive song, flirts with the human detective, who breaks out in a nervous, lustful sweat.

Reviewers say that *Who Framed Roger Rabbit?* broke a lot of boundaries previously unbroken in Hollywood moviemaking. The boundary between human actors and animated characters had been breached before, but never with such amazing skill.[16] Certainly, though, no human being had ever been so sexually aroused by a cartoon character on screen before as was the human detective being melodically seduced by the wife of another cartoon character.

Speaking of Disney, Touchstone, Eisner and their Hollywood aristocracy, Knight says their attitude about making films is deplorable.

> You have to wonder what is making them tick. Why are they motivated to get down and dirty when they already have a glittering empire where there is infinite room to expand with more new products and the old as well? Certainly there isn't an overload of wholesome product out there.
>
> Anytime Disney does something even remotely family friendly, it's gobbled up by a grateful public. So why they continue down this path of anti-family, pro-promiscuity in their films is beyond belief.[17]

If Walt Disney Could Speak

Knight is not alone in his criticism of the new Disney thrust. Some old-timers feel that if Walt were still alive, he'd do to Eisner and friends what Eisner and friends did to his studio crew—and directors like Scorsese wouldn't be able to get past the front gate. Walt would be incensed, supposedly, at the level of family-degrading, sexually implicit and explicit movies being made.

This is reinforced dramatically by Walt's attitude about sex, according to Leonard Mosely.

> He believed unmarried females should always behave like well-brought-up young ladies and never act cheaply with men. He was of the opinion that no decent girl should ever marry before the age of 25, and then not before consulting her parents. Nor should she ever, no matter what her age, surrender her virginity to anyone out of wedlock, even if she had fallen in love.[18]

Walt Disney was especially negative toward sexual promiscuity. During the production of *Snow White*, there was intense concentration at the studio. As a thank you to all for their efforts, Disney invited the whole company to a getaway weekend at a lakeside hotel.

The champagne flowed, and so did the passions of Walt's staff. A Disney animator recalled what followed:

> By the end of the first evening, something snapped. Playsuits flew out of windows. There were naked swim parties in the pool. Inhibitions, respectability and tensions vanished with each new bottle of champagne. Everybody got drunk. It developed into what was

practically an orgy, with animators reeling around tipsily and staggering off to sleep with whomever took their fancy.[19]

When Disney saw what was happening, he was horrified. He didn't even stay for the rest of the weekend and never again mentioned the party.[20]

The Former Animators Do Speak

Though the new Disney was piling up many friends and supporters, there were other voices from the past—voices from veteran Disney animators who saw their own work copied and presented as new.

They were particularly upset with the studio's new use of computer animation. The feeling of the old Disney men was that Disney had sold out its creative legacy—the hand-drawn animation in the service of great storytelling. Disney's new efforts, they accused, were merely "thinly disguised" rehashes of the originals.[21]

Eliot puts it this way:

> One longtime Disney animator claimed that *Honey, I Shrunk the Kids* with its larger and smaller motif, was really nothing more than a remake of *Alice in Wonderland*. Eisner's sidekick, Katzenberg, couldn't resist telling interviewers how much *Beauty and the Beast* "owed" to the look, style and approach of *Pinocchio*.[22]

Disney's apparent assault on the family and, in particular, marriage (which is illustrated for the most part as cumbersome, unimportant and a nuisance when it comes to sexual fulfillment), is well documented in its films—and well disputed in Scripture.

By way of contrast, theologian J.I. Packer says that marriage is meant by God to be a permanent covenant.

> Marriage was ordained for the mutual help of husband and wife, for the increase of mankind with a legitimate issue, and of the church with a holy seed, and for preventing of uncleanness (sexual immorality). By using Christ's relationship to His church to illustrate what Christian marriage ought to be, Paul highlights the husband's special responsibility as his wife's leader and protector, and the wife's calling to accept her husband in that role (Ephesians 5:21-33).

> The distinction of roles does not, however, imply that the wife is an inferior person. As God's image-bearers, the husband and the wife have equal dignity and value, and they are to fulfill their role relationship on the basis of a mutual respect that is rooted in recognition of this fact.[23]

But, as we will see, the Disney corporation in the 1990s brings with it an entire array of anti-family, anti-Bible and decidedly anti-Christian entertainment.

Endnotes

1. Richard Holliss and Brian Sibley, *The Disney Studio Story* (New York: Crown, 1988), p. 108.

2. Ibid.

3. Michael Medved, *Hollywood vs. America* (New York: Harper Perennial, 1992), p. 96.

4. Interview with Robert Knight, 1996, on file with the author.

5. Ibid.

6. Ibid.

7. Holliss and Sibley, p. 108.

8. Knight interview.

9. Billy Graham, *Storm Warnings* (Dallas, TX: Word, 1992), pp. 22-23.

10. James Dobson, *Children at Risk: The Battle for the Hearts and Minds of Our Kids* (Dallas, TX: Word, 1990), p. 55.

11. Medved, p. 44.

12. Ibid.

13. Ibid., p. 39.

14. Texe Marrs, personal interview, 1996, on file with author.

15. Medved, p. 44.

16. *Cinemania* (Redmond, WA: Microsoft, 1995), CD-ROM.

17. Knight interview.

18. Leonard Mosley, *Disney's World* (New York: Stein & Day, 1985), p. 252.

19. Ibid., p. 166.

20. Ibid., p. 168.

21. Marc Eliot, *Walt Disney: Hollywood's Dark Prince* (New York: Carol Publishing, 1993), p. 279.

22. Ibid.

23. J.I. Packer, *A Concise Theology* (Wheaton, IL: Tyndale, 1993), pp. 229-230.

What the Bible Says about Sexual Immorality

Marriage is honourable in all, and the bed undefiled: but whoremongers and adulterers God will judge. (Hebrews 13:4)

But the fearful, and unbelieving, and the abominable, and murderers, and **whoremongers,** *and sorcerers, and idolaters, and all liars, shall have their part in the lake which burneth with fire and brimstone: which is the second death.* (Revelation 21:8, emphasis added)

Flee fornication. Every sin that a man doeth is without the body; but he that committeth fornication sinneth against his own body. What? know ye not that your body is the temple of the Holy Ghost which is in you, which ye have of God, and ye are not your own? For ye are bought with a price: therefore glorify God in your body. (1 Corinthians 6:18-20)

Know ye not that the unrighteous shall not inherit the kingdom of God? Be not deceived: neither **fornicators,** *nor idolaters, nor* **adulterers,** *nor* **effeminate, nor abusers of themselves with mankind,** *nor thieves, nor covetous, nor drunkards, nor revilers, nor extortioners, shall inherit the kingdom of God. And such were some of you: but ye are washed, but ye are sanctified, but ye are justified in the name of the Lord Jesus, and by the Spirit of our God.* (1 Corinthians 6:9-11, emphasis added)

Chapter 6

Disney's Sickness of the Spirit

> *Humanity, as history informs us, changes very slowly in character and basic interests. [People] never cease to be fascinated by their own powers and passions, their base or noble emotions, their faiths and struggles against triumph and handicap—all the things that make them laugh and weep and comfort one another in love and sacrifice out of the depths of their being.*
>
> *—Walt Disney*

Successes were mounting for Touchstone Pictures to the point that it was overshadowing its parent corporation. It was only reasonable that Michael Eisner would want to duplicate what Touchstone was doing.

In 1988, Eisner did just that. He called yet another Paramount alumnus, Ricardo Mestres, to take charge of Walt Disney Corporation's newest studio, Hollywood Pictures.

In 1990, under the Hollywood Pictures banner, Eisner reaped a monster hit with the premiering of *Pretty Woman*. It was the story of a prostitute (Julia Roberts) who is hired by a business mogul (Richard Gere) for a week-long sexual escapade. The outcome was a fairy tale romance. Prince Charming rescued Snow White and the happy couple drove off together in the prince's limo.

The story line was unalloyed fantasy. Not very many Hollywood streetwalkers look like Julia Roberts—or are as wholesome and clean. And not very many Johns are as rich, respectable and harmless as Richard Gere.

Prostitutes have become fair game for predators who avail themselves of their services and dispose of them like used tissues as one very brief scene in the movie depicts. The bodies of young women of the night continue to litter our back alleys, our river beds and our secluded wooded areas. To solve these crimes sometimes requires a sophisticated Green River Task Force such as Washington state set up to solve a string of vicious, brutal murders levied against Northwest hookers.

And what of those who frequent these prostitutes? Statistics confirm that the majority are married, middle-aged and responsibly employed.

The Wrong Message

The danger of *Pretty Woman*, though, may be

in the seemingly clean and virtuous way the characters are depicted and how their indecent liaisons lead to a happily-ever-after conclusion.

In today's world of indiscriminate sex, leading to dangerous and even deadly consequences due to the AIDS epidemic, *Pretty Woman* seems to be the HIV's chief spin doctor. Conservative figures suggest that over half of the prostitutes in any given city at any given time are infected with HIV, so that involvment with a prostitute carries tremendous risk of contracting the deadly disease. Normal, even paranormal, success stories which fail to slow consequences send the wrong message and condone the practice of prostitution and illicit sex.

Ironically, Hollywood sends a double message: Sex is okay, even applaudable, but drug use isn't. In *Pretty Woman*, for example, there is a scene where Julia Roberts is hiding something from Richard Gere. Gere tells her that if it's drugs she can take a hike. Roberts, it turns out, is holding dental floss. The message here is that if you want a rich and powerful guy like Gere, don't do drugs.[1]

Along with the adulation of sex, the film is packed with profanity and innuendo, all wrapped up in a little neat package of power, money, corporate shenanigans and fantasy dates with a prostitute worth a million dollars.

Other Disney films with the Hollywood Pictures label include *The Hand That Rocks the Cradle*, starring Rebecca De Mornay as a broke, homeless and psychotic baby sitter obsessed with revenge. The film is packed with violence, horror, profanity and sex.

In addition, Hollywood Pictures churned out *The Marrying Man*, starring Alec Baldwin and Kim Basinger, whose on-screen sexual sizzle was almost completely overshadowed by their torrid, off-screen affair. *Premiere Magazine* reported that Baldwin and Basinger fell deeply and passionately into love and lust, and that the filming of many a scene was delayed while they "lingered" in their mobile homes.[2]

But Hollywood Pictures also spit out films like Eddie Murphy's *The Distinguished Gentleman*, laced with sexual allusion; *Consenting Adults*, the story of wife swapping in suburbia; *Encino Man*, complete with nitwit ideology, sexual permissiveness and drug abuse; and *Born Yesterday*, starring Don Johnson and his on-again, off-again wife Melanie Griffith, in a tale about a tycoon trying to educate his adulterous mistress.

On Television Too

Not to be outdone by the big screen, the Disney empire in 1990 premiered on NBC the horribly received teenage musical, "Hull High." It was a veritable raunchfest of jiggling high school girls, lusty female teachers and more than eager male students. The studio called it an innocent "kids' fantasy."[3]

The Disney corporate mind-set was at play in another of its television efforts, the widely popular "Empty Nest." In one episode lauding single parenthood, daughter Barbara wanted to get pregnant from a sperm bank.

"Why should I obligate a guy for the rest of his life when I only need him for an hour?" she shockingly asks.[4]

The Walt Disney Corporation has brought to the public via its "adult" studios an overt and constant accentuation of sex. Many concerned church leaders consider it a tragedy and a travesty.

"With Disney [corporation], there's obviously an increasing emphasis on nonfamily-oriented entertainment," says D. James Kennedy, noted author and pastor. "Like so many, I grew up with Walt Disney. He presented sometimes the only family entertainment available. It's very distressing to see [the corporation] moving in a direction like this."[5]

Hollywood's argument is that they're not trying to lead people by the nose. They are not attempting to force their agendas on anyone. They merely make movies that reflect society. Kennedy disagrees.

> That is mostly untrue. No doubt gutter language and toilet language are in this country. Everyone of us has heard some samples. But America is not made up of gutters and toilets. If you fix your camera on just those kinds of things, that's what you're going to get. . . .

[Hollywood] picks some negative and unwholesome part of society and fixes its cameras on it. That simply popularizes it and makes it more commonplace.[6]

The Danger of Desensitization

Kennedy says the key term is *desensitization*. He points out that the Hollywood elite, including those at the helm of the Disney corporation, are doing just that to America's families.

"We're being desensitized to every kind of evil imaginable," declares Kennedy concerning what Disney and others in Hollywood are promoting. He continues:

> There's a little poem that puts it very well: "Vice is a monster of so frightful mien, / As to be hated needs but to be seen; / Yet seen too oft, familiar with her face, / We first endure, then pity, then embrace" [Alexander Pope].
>
> That's desensitization. We're being desensitized to the homosexual lifestyle, to pornography, to profanity, to blasphemy. We're being desensitized to every kind of immorality. These [entertainment] programs compete with each other to find a more perverse, distorted arrangement to present before the public.

People are being deceived and misled. People are being desensitized to worse and worse things. I think somebody needs to call [the entertainment industry] on that.[7]

Kennedy is particularly disappointed that Walt Disney Corporation would go in this direction. He declares some of the product coming out of Disney so unthinkable it's shocking.

"When the American public wakes up to what Disney is doing, they are going to be very offended," Kennedy says.

When people begin to realize that these terrible things are coming from the Disney organization, Disney will find its audience plummeting. Disney studios have been held up as the very height of wholesome family entertainment. I'm afraid Disney is in for a big fall.[8]

Besides Touchstone and Hollywood Pictures, the Walt Disney Corporation also owns Miramax, a highly successful production organization. Miramax too has quite a track record of highly questionable films.

New Lows in Sex and Violence

Pulp Fiction, with John Travolta, brought indiscriminate, bawdy sex and extreme violence to new lows. *The Crow,* a tale of a murdered rock musician who rises from the dead, was a foray into reincarnation and the occult. As the former rock star seeks vengeance on those who killed him, he is guided by an occultic black crow. The picture paints a horrid image of satanic influence, abetted by Brandon Lee's death just before the filming was completed.

Interestingly, Miramax participated in the 1994 Los Angeles Gay and Lesbian Film and Video Festival. The company brought an unedited copy of *Pulp Fiction,* depicting full frontal nudity, to the screening room. The picture, which actor Bruce Willis described in the grossest of terms, won an award at the festival.

There have been lesser-known Miramax treasures. *Clerks* touted graphic language describing sexual acts. *Fresh* glorified the lifestyle of a drug dealer. *Snapper* was about an unmarried pregnant girl with highly sexual undertones. In *Sirens,* a liberal British minister and his wife are seduced by an Australian artist and his three nude models. *The Pope Must Die* was a yarn about a Roman Catholic priest who illicitly fathers a heavy metal rock star. He then becomes Pope, complete with sexy nuns, and is found gorging himself on communion wafers. *Exotica* is a lurid tale of an obsessed patron in a stripper bar who can't take his eyes off a stripper dressed as a Catholic school girl.

Quite apart from the sex-saturated pictures being ground out by the Disney corporation's subsidiaries, even the cartoons are sexier. Robert Knight, Director of Cultural Studies for the Family Research Council, says a comparison of present and earlier Disney animation tells the tale. "Look at the Little Mermaid, at Jasmine in Aladdin, at Pocahontas. . . . The current Disney heroines have a bust line, and they manage to show lots of cleavage."

Knight quotes a Disney spokesperson who admits, "Yes, we've made sure they [the characters] were sexualized." Knight adds:

> There's really no reason to do that in a movie for children, but Disney knows that pubescent kids start noticing that kind of stuff. And I do see it as part of a larger agenda going on in this country through Hollywood, [the schools], the media. . . . That agenda is the sexualizing of [our] children.[9]

New Highs in Homosexual Realism

Not only has Miramax's production been laden with gratuitous sex but, as we have seen, some of the pictures have ridiculed the Christian faith. Still others evidence a predilection toward homosexuality. A case in point is *Priest*. The movie tells the story of five Roman Catholic priests. One is involved in a heated homosexual affair, one is having sex with his housekeeper, another is an alcoholic, the fourth is an uncompassionate bishop, the last is a psychotic. The

American Family Association's *AFA Journal*, calls *Priest* a "depiction of gay sex that by all accounts is one of the most realistic ever filmed outside the world of pornography."[10] One scene in the film portrays a priest who becomes sexually stimulated at the sight of Jesus Christ hanging on the cross.[11]

Miramax's bag of tricks contains two more controversial films not yet produced. One, *Chasing Amy*, is about a man who falls hopelessly in love with a lesbian. The other, *Dogma*, is a treatment of Christian mythology that, according to *Variety* magazine, "will take its place in the Miramax library of controversial religion-themed films alongside *Priest* and *The Advocate*."[12]

With Miramax splattering so much ribald debauchery and salacious indulgence all over the Disney corporation, the question arises, Why? Why produce and distribute movies that create ill-will and storms of controversy from a supposed majority of North American households?

Miramax president Mark Gill says it's simple. Sex sells. He's not even averse to spicing up his ads by touting plot twists that may not actually play an important part in the film.

"We spend a lot of time making movies look more provocative than they really are," Gill said at a recent Toronto International Film Festival symposium. "Our cheap cliché is 'Sex, betrayal, murder.' You'll see a lot of women with no clothes on their backs in our ads. We'll put a gun in if we can. It works. You can scorn me for this, but it works."[13]

The Disney corporation seems to have discovered something else that works: how sordid the director's reputation is. I referred to Martin Scorsese in chapter 5. To direct *Powder*, the story of a boy with occultic, New Age powers, the corporation chose Victor Salva. According to the American Family Association's *AFA Journal*, Salva is a convicted child molester who videotaped himself having oral sex with a twelve-year-old actor in one of his earlier movies. The incident apparently mushroomed when the boy, Nathan Winters, now twenty, went public with the story.[14]

Salva was convicted on two felony counts of lewd and lascivious conduct and having oral copulation with a person under fourteen. He was convicted on three counts of procuring a child for pornography. He served a total of fifteen months.

In response to the animosity over the selection of Salva, Disney spokesperson John Dreyer seemed puzzled. Reportedly he asked, "What's the point other than you want to make headlines?"[15]

If Salva made headlines, another Disney/Miramax release promises to do much, much more. Too hot for even Miramax, Disney set up a separate distribution company to market the unrated shocker, *Kids*.

Following its showing at the Cannes (France) Film Festival in May, 1995, news services reported serious rumblings from the entertainment community. People were branding it "kiddie porn." A Reuters News Service report has this to say about the movie and its plot:

> *Kids* opens with the pubescent lead, a self-styled virgin surgeon, deeply kissing a 14-year-old girl as a giant teddy bear looms in the background.
>
> His seduction attempt is successful and related in coarse and graphic detail to a friend moments later—a taste of the coarse exchanges that run through the film.
>
> Through one of the boy's conquests, we discover he is infected with the HIV virus [sic] that causes AIDS. The girl later tracks him down, only to find him making love to another virgin.
>
> Some critics dubbed the film voyeuristic and gratuitously violent both in its dialogue and action.[16]

The Associated Press reported *Kids* in Cannes this way:

> The festival got a taste of explicit teenage sex courtesy of Walt Disney. [The film] begins with close up shots of Telly, played by skateboarder and first-time actor Lee Fitzpatrick, deflowering another conquest. "Virgins. I love 'em. No diseases," says Telly, who bounds

off to join his buddies to the wail of rap metal by the Beastie Boys.[17]

The movie also depicts the painfully long rape sequence of a teenage girl who passes out, high on drugs.[18]

As shocking as *Kids* is, the film is upstaged by its director, Larry Clark. Clark is described as a "photographer of the adolescent demimonde."[19] Clark had the honor of being featured in an issue of *Gayme* Magazine, which caters to pedophiles and features nude and seminude photographs of boys. According to *Gayme*, Clark's projects deal with the world of boy prostitutes and drug addicts. "Clark has always been a participant-observer in the scenes he photographed," the article says.[20] In the magazine Clark is shown nude showering with young boys.

The magazine goes on to paint a further disturbing picture of the Disney-associated filmmaker. In some of his photographs he focuses on teen suicide. One photo, according to the publication, reveals a teenage boy's genitalia and shows the boy with a large pistol in his mouth.[21]

With the Disney corporation setting the pace with sexually explicit and sexually deviate films, one would expect its reputation among North American Christians to be irrevocably harmed. Such seems not to be the case.

Recently, for example, Trinity Broadcasting Network aired a program featuring rock music evangelist Jeff Fenholt. Fenholt was at Disney World in Orlando beckoning his television audience to "come to Disney World to praise the Lord." Both Disneyland in California and Disney World in Florida remain perennial favorites of Christians. They still feel the Walt Disney Corporation is Hollywood's only champion of family values.

"They don't get it yet," says Robert Knight, concerning Christians who continue to patronize the Disney empire. "They don't understand that they're supporting [a subversive] agenda that's aimed directly at them." Knight goes on:

> The best outcome in this whole thing would be for Disney to go back to doing what it does best—producing family-friendly fare—and abandon its radicalism. The Christian view should always be to convert rather than to harm.
>
> The next best thing would be for people to withhold their consumer purchases to the point where Disney corporation has a change in management.[22]

Some Christian groups *are* doing something about what many refer to as "the Disney betrayal." The Florida Baptist State Convention, at its annual convocation in 1995, called for a boycott of Disney theme parks, Disney products and Disney films. The American Family Association has endorsed the boycott. Says Donald E. Wildmon, its president:

> We applaud the decision of the Florida Baptist State Convention to encourage its members to boycott Disney parks and products. We hope that the entire Southern Baptist Convention will get behind the boycott and let American families know that they can no longer trust Disney to provide wholesome family entertainment.[23]

More recently, after expressing disappointment with Disney, the Southern Baptist Convention, representing 16 million evangelicals, passed a resolution as follows:

> That we encourage Southern Baptists to give serious and prayerful reconsideration to their purchase and support of Disney products; and to boycott Disney if it continues its policy.[24]

The Assemblies of God, too, have taken a stand:

> On behalf of nearly 12,000 Assemblies of God congregations, Rev. George Wood, General Secretary of the denomination, cancelled the church's chapter in Disney's Magic Kingdom Club.
> Citing the increasing promotion of ho-

mosexuality by Disney (i.e. Disney-owned Hyperion Press's book, *Growing Up Gay in America,* the homosexually-oriented movie, *Priest,* and Gay and Lesbian days at Disney World) as the reason for the cancellation, Wood sent Disney the bad news via a letter dated May 17, 1996.

"For over 20 years, our denominational headquarters has participated with confidence in the Magic Kingdom Club," Wood wrote Disney Chairman Michael Eisner. "We have promoted visits to the Disney theme parks by providing membership cards to hundreds of our employees as well as thousands of our churches and 2 1/2 million members as places they can visit knowing their family moral values will not be impinged. That support is no longer possible."[25]

More than fifteen Florida lawmakers have condemned the Walt Disney Corporation for extending health insurance to partners of homosexual employees, complaining that the move endorses an unhealthy, unnatural lifestyle.

The lawmakers told the Disney organization in a letter that the move was "a big mistake both morally and financially" that would alienate families. Said Representative Bob Brooks, a doctor and an infectious disease specialist: "I feel this policy is headed in the wrong direction. In the long run, it will result in an increased number of AIDS cases."[26]

But as we will see, protests of Disney's increased acceptance of pornography, teenage sex and homosexuality falls on deaf ears as the organization comes out of the closet.

Endnotes

1. Michael Medved, *Hollywood vs. America* (New York: Harper Perennial, 1992), p. 337.

2. Roger Ebert, *Cinemania* (Redmond, WA: Microsoft, 1995), CD-ROM.

3. Medved, p. 110.

4. Ibid., p. 144.

5. D. James Kennedy, personal interview, 1996, on file with author.

6. Ibid.

7. Ibid.

8. Ibid.

9. Robert Knight, personal interview, 1996, on file with author.

10. *AFA Journal*, May 1995, p. 9.

11. Michael Medved, "The New Disney: The Offenses Grow," *Citizen Magazine*, December 1995, p. 2. quoted in Internet: Newsprint 2.1, Openwin Library 3, ROOT@WMM, Christopher Corbett, "The New Disney."

12. John Davis, "Amy Lands at Miramax," *Daily Variety*, November 3, 1995, p. 3, quoted in *AFA Journal*, November/December, 1995, p. 11.

13. *AFA Journal,* November/Decemer 1995; *The Washington Times,* October 25, 1995, p. 2.

14. *AFA Journal,* November/December 1995, p. 11.

15. Dave Geisler, "Christians Launch Disney Boycott," *Charisma Christian Life Magazine,* October 1995, p. 34.

16. Reuters news report from Disney access Web Page, Internet, action index, December 1995.

17. *AFA Journal,* July 1995, p. 9; Associated Press, May 22, 1995.

18. Reuters, Disney Web Page.

19. D.H. Mader, "Lust and Death," *Gayme Magazine,* 1995, vol. 2.2, p. 3.

20. Ibid., pp. 28-31.

21. Reuters, Disney Web Page.

22. Knight interview.

23. American Family Association press release, November 16, 1995.

24. SBC Bulletin, June 1996, p. 6.

25. Juleen Turnage, Secretary of Public Relations, Assemblies of God, media release, July 1996.

26. "Florida Lawmakers Blast Disney for Gay Policy," *The Clarion-Ledger* (Jackson, MS) October 19, 1995, p. 8A.

What the Bible Says about Practicing Homosexuals

Thou shalt not lie with mankind, as with womankind: it is abomination. (Leviticus 18:22)

If a man also lie with mankind, as he lieth with a woman, both of them have committed an abomination: they shall surely be put to death; their blood shall be upon them. (Leviticus 20:13)

There shall be no whore of the daughters of Israel, nor a sodomite of the sons of Israel. Thou shalt not bring the hire of a whore, or the price of a dog, into the house of the LORD thy God for any vow: for even both these are abomination unto the LORD thy God. (Deuteronomy 23:17-18)

For this cause God gave them up unto vile affections: for even their women did change the natural use into that which is against nature: And likewise also the men, leaving the natural use of the woman, burned in their lust one toward another; men with men working that which is unseemly, and receiving in themselves that recompense of their error which was meet. . . .

Who knowing the judgment of God, that they which commit such things are worthy of death, not only do the same, but have pleasure in them that do them. (Romans 1:26-27, 32)

Chapter 7

Mickey Comes Out of the Closet

The era we are living in today is a dream come true.

—Walt Disney

By the mid-1990s Walt Disney Corporation had become one of the most powerful and influential entertainment organizations in the world. With the enormous revenue brought in by its theme parks, for example, it could absorb any box office disasters. And Michael Eisner had his share of them.

It was no secret within the Hollywood community that Disney corporation was looking around for another company to devour. But the general public was amazed when, on July 31, 1995, Disney announced its plans to merge with Capital Cities/ABC at a value of approximately $19 billion.

In a joint statement, Michael Eisner and Thomas Murphy, CEO of Capital Cities/ABC, said the opportunities were unlimited.

> The combined company will become a vital and dynamic force in the entertainment and media business, reaching family audiences worldwide and providing them with unparalleled news, information and entertainment both inside and outside the home. . . . The combined enterprise will be better equipped to grow, to provide valuable services for our viewers, listeners, readers, sports fans and vacationers, and to capture the imagination for future generations.[1]

Stockholders reeled from the news. Wall Street moguls positioned themselves to cash in on the venture. And likely Glitterville's elite, behind closed doors, were snickering at the deal they were sure Uncle Walt would never have countenanced.

Yet Another Surprise

Meanwhile, the American consumer was in for yet another surprise. The Disney corporation was coming out of the closet. For years, insiders understood the corporation to be increasingly homosexually oriented—not unlike other major

Hollywood studios. But when Disney gave in to gay lobbying forces and extended health insurance to partners of homosexual workers, North America's religious community was generally dismayed.

For two years Disney's own homosexual union, the Lesbian and Gay United Employees (LEAGUE), had been pressing the organization for these insurance benefits.[2] In April, 1994, the union presented the Disney corporation with a detailed analysis of the fiscal and social ramifications of homosexual partner health benefits. LEAGUE rebutted concerns about high costs of the coverage by citing a nationwide study that found employers didn't boost their costs by extending benefits to homosexuals. Its report told of tangible gains made by companies that had adopted similar health plans, including Viacom, Time/Warner and MCA/Universal.[3]

In a rebuke to Disney's pro-gay decision, Traditional Values Coalition chairman Lou Sheldon cites another study.

"Homosexuality is like a revolving door," Sheldon says, referring to a survey that only twenty percent of all homosexuals are gay for life. "The remaining 80 percent are merely passing through and would never actually remain gay long enough to enjoy the benefits of the Disney package. So Disney has sold its image for not even a bowl of pottage. This is certainly not the organization Walt Disney founded."[4]

The powerful Florida Baptist State Convention evidently had similar feelings. It saw Disney's agreeing to cover homosexuals in their insurance program as tantamount to approval of that lifestyle.

"Historically Disney has reinforced America's values," said convention spokeswoman Barbara Denman. "We noticed there had been an erosion in its moral leadership."[5]

Gay Theme Nights in the Parks

In addition, Denman says, the Convention is opposed to homosexual and lesbian theme nights at Disney's parks. It also opposes the kinds of motion pictures Disney is producing through its various studios such as Miramax.

John Dreyer, speaking for the Disney corporation, says the company regrets the stand of the Florida Baptists:

> The standard against which our commitment to family entertainment should be measured is the value and high quality of Disney-branded family entertainment that we produce. . . . [Disney] is the world's leader in producing entertainment for the entire family.[6]

But Dreyer was in no mood to back down on the medical, vision and dental insurance decision for same sex domestic partners. "We felt we should bring [these benefits] in line with our nondiscrimination policy," he said. When asked why the health benefits would not be extended to unmarried heterosexual domestic partners, Dreyer was emphatic. "We're just not going to extend it, and we're not really interested in debating it."[7]

To fully understand Disney corporation's position on the medical insurance issue, one has to know the corporation's makeup. According to Los Angeles-based *Buzz* Magazine, the "happiest place on earth," as Disney likes to bill itself, is also one of the gayest. "There are hordes of gay and lesbian people at Disney," says Garrett Hicks, an openly homosexual employee there.[8]

In the past few years, Disney has earned a justified reputation as a haven for lesbians and homosexuals. This is true not simply on the creative side, as one might expect, but in Disney's hallowed mahogany row as well.

According to *Buzz* Magazine, homosexual executives in the Disney organization include Hollywood Pictures production vice-president Lauren Lloyd; studio producer Laurence Mark and supervising animator Andreas Deja, who was responsible for the Gaston character in *Beauty and the Beast*. They include Steven Fields, vice-president at Disney's interactive division; Rick Leed, head of production who oversees Disney's hit sitcom, "Home Improvement"; and senior vice-president Thomas Schumacher, one of the described "guiding lights" behind *Lion King*.[9]

A Subliminal Attraction

Schumacher confirms that there are a number of homosexuals at Disney at various levels. He believes they are drawn to the company because of what they pick up subliminally from the Disney cartoons.

"Thematically, the animated films promote the right to be who you are," Schumacher says, "and not to change for anyone else. The characters make their own family. They bond and have close friends. They grow up and grow old together. Anyone who is disenfranchised is touched by that."[10]

When LEAGUE was first formed, the Disney corporation refused to let them identify themselves by the Disney name. At the 1993 gay march on Washington, LEAGUE had prepared a banner that read, "Lesbian and Gay United Employees . . . part of the family at the Walt Disney Company." A corporate directive demanded them to cover up the reference to Walt Disney. Less than a year later, Disney gave the union permission to identify the employment status of LEAGUE members with the Disney name on its banner, as long as the banner stated that there was no official Disney endorsement or participation.[11]

At Orlando's Epcot Center, Jimi Ziehr, a training coordinator, says homosexuals outnumber straights at one of the operations. Quips Ziehr, "There's nothing in the closet at Guest Relations."[12]

Does Disney have an official position on the migration of homosexuals to the "House that Walt Built"? Perhaps the answer has come from senior Disney publicist, Richard Jordan. "Someone in personnel must have a sweet tooth," he says.[13]

If anyone is to be thanked or reviled for the pro-homosexual temperament at Disney, it is the former head of the Disney film entertainment division, Jeffrey Katzenberg. He himself is heterosexual but sympathetic to the gay agenda.

"Katzenberg was very sensitive to gay issues," says Deja, "and it was always very comfortable to work with him. He was fine with a lot of things that concern gay people. . . . I think [that] created a good atmosphere for anybody who was gay at the studio."[14]

Katzenberg is now gone from Disney with more than hard feelings between him and one-time boss and friend, Eisner. He now is part of the Dream Works organization with Steven Spielberg and the openly homosexual David Geffen.[15] Reports have it that the pro-gay Hollywood golden boy threatened to sue Disney and Eisner for $300 million unless they could reach a last-minute settlement. Disney corporation is of the opinion that Katzenberg is owed only about $100 million.[16]

With Katzenberg gone, Disney has shelved plans for a movie version of the homosexual-themed musical, *Falsettos*. But not for lack of interest in the subject. "Jeffrey Katzenberg understood the political nature of the issues," says Schumacher. "Michael [Eisner] is respectful, but he doesn't grasp the complexity of the problem."[17]

No Changes at ABC

When Eisner gobbled up ABC, he said he saw no reason to change any of ABC's programming. The network's strategy, he said, was working.

Words like that from the CEO of a major family-oriented studio sounded a bit incongruous. ABC's "NYPD Blue" and its "real life" portrayal of police officers as foul-mouthed, vulgar-acting, sex-hungry beef on the hoof is hardly family entertainment.

In addition, the ABC that Eisner says he won't change has had a long and unenviable history of pro-homosexual shows. For example, in the scene on the "Thirtysomething" series, two male characters appeared in bed together, talking about the one-night stand they've just had.[18]

Later the network aired the same two characters exchanging a passionate midnight kiss at a New Year's party. That episode cost ABC more than $500,000 in advertising earnings.

With so much money—the industry's lifeblood—draining away on homosexually oriented movies and TV programming, why does a network like ABC insist on running such stuff? Robert Iger, president of ABC Entertainment during that time, said the sum and substance reflected his "social and creative responsibilities."[19]

Michael Medved points out that this attitude is commonplace in the entertainment industry:

> While "gay control" of the movie business is a myth, gay influence is very much a reality. No one could deny that the formidable gay presence in the entertainment business encourages industry leaders to take a far more sympathetic view of homosexuality than does the public at large.[20]

Some Seepage at the Disney Corporation

With influential homosexuals making decisions at Disney, it would seem only natural for the gay agenda to seep into the so-called family films. It has.

For example, in *Aladdin* the Genie gurgles to his young master, "I'm getting fond of you, kid—not that I want to pick out curtains or anything." Also in *Aladdin* is the campy, homosexual-like performance of Iago, the parrot. And the Genie itself turns into a stereotypical swishy clothier.

In *Beauty and the Beast,* the conceited Gaston throws his legs over the arms of his chair and expounds, "I do all my decorating with antlers." One of the homosexual workers on the film said that Gaston was modeled after "preening West Hollywood muscle clones."[21] (Next to San Francisco, West Hollywood may be the homosexual capital of the world.)

An opinion editorial in the *Boston Globe* complained that Scar, the deviant, conniving lion in *Lion King* "speaks in supposed gay clichés" and ambles with "effeminate gestures."[22]

Officials at Disney worried that the "gay shtick" in some of its animated movies was going too far. But the scenes stayed in, much to the delectation of Disney's homosexual cadre.

Another of Disney's ventures is its own book publishing company, Hyperion, named after Walt's beloved studio situated on the street of the same name. Far from family-oriented, Hyperion is a haven for what some call antifamily and antibiblical intellectualization via the printed word. One of the most infamous books to come out of Hyperion is the 1995 book, *Growing Up Gay in America*, by "Funny Gay Males."

"Disney is becoming more bold in its promotion of the homosexual agenda," says Donald E. Wildmon, American Family Association president. "More and more families are waking up to the fact that Disney is using its huge influence with America's children and families to suggest that dangerous, perverted sexual behavior is okay."[23]

According to Hyperion's director of publicity, Lisa Kitei, *Growing Up Gay* (which has been accused of being no more than a recruitment weapon to entice boys into the homosexual lifestyle), debunks some ridiculous myths and creates a few of their own.

"Funny Gay Males" traces the gay boy's progress through life. Where do gay children come from? Is it nature? Is it nurture? If straight kids are found in the cabbage patch, are gay kids discovered under the arugula? Or are we gay kids simply delivered by pink flamingoes?

Claiming that gay boys are different even in infancy, when they would have preferred lavender blankets rather than the traditional blue, the authors present gay versions of fairy tales and nursery rhymes.[24]

Growing Up Gay in America could be no less than a no-holds-barred guided missile aimed right at the hearts of America's children. For example, the authors state that a gay kid is not just a child who will one day turn into a gay adult.

> We're learning that the gay child—even before he begins socializing with other gay adults—is already sharing likes, dislikes, interests and outlooks with a worldwide culture of which he's only vaguely aware. In short, we guessed that something was cooking even before we started baking. We knew we were different the first time we noticed Lee Majors was wearing tight

pants on the Big Valley. We knew we were different the first time we found ourselves daintily shaking a packet of sweetener between our thumb and middle finger just like Aunt Marge. And we knew we were different that first summer we wanted to send a postcard to Johnny saying, "I wish you were here," and the boy in question lived right next door.[25]

If *Growing Up Gay in America* is just a bit shocking to both the mainstream and the religious community, you ain't seen nothin' yet. Disney has also published the autobiography of transvestite super-model RuPaul called, aptly enough, *Lettin' It All Hang Out.*

Hyped by Disney's Hyperion as a "crossover, cross-dressing sensation," the publishing company says he—uh, she—uh, well, RuPaul is actually a "role model"—pointing to the drag queen as a young man who grew up in poverty and rose through the ranks to a life of fame, riches, success and glamour. Hyperion says that his—uh, her—uh, RuPaul's autobiography is a story of inspiration and charm, of love and humor, of dedication and success.[26]

The RuPaul book is not really an autobiography in the purest sense of the word. It's more of a how-to manual for other aspiring drag queens. In Chapter 1, for example, the transvestite says the first thing to do is say a little prayer. "I go to my vanity and pray to the gods of Charles Revson, Max Factor, Flori Roberts and all the other patron saints of beauty," he/she says.[27]

Then the queen of drag describes in detail how he/she shaves. "I shave my face closely so that if by chance that evening a fan should brush a hand against my cheek, they'll feel the silky smoothness of a baby's bottom."[28]

From bras, hose, spiked heels and more, Ru-Paul gives the hopeful transvestite every imaginable tool to transform a male into a female, then back again.

RuPaul lists thirty-five nonnegotiable things one needs to be a successful drag queen. Suggestions include a flawless, fierce attitude, an assortment of make-up, push-up bra, gym socks rolled up tight for breasts, hot pants, mini-dress, perfume (RuPaul suggests "Whore—for she who is") and positive love energy.

But wait, there's more. He/she even gives tips on what the well-stocked "drag purse" should contain and includes compact, lipstick, condoms, tic tacs and mace.[29]

Finally, it was bound to happen. Disney's syndication arm, Buena Vista Television, has reportedly spoken with the transvestite about hosting a late-night talk show. According to the report in *Variety*, one of the movie industry's trade papers, the late-night show is but one offer RuPaul has considered. A source at Buena Vista confirmed the negotiations with the drag queen.[30]

What Can a Christian Do?

An editorial in *Christianity Today,* the well-known evangelical fortnightly, offers perceptive counsel. Roberto Rivera, a fellow with the Wilberforce Forum, says this:

> Before we boycott Disney or anyone else to affirm our Christian moral perspective, and even before we develop a philosophy of what we can expect of our non-Christian neighbors, we must also ask: What ought we to expect of ourselves as a Christian community?
>
> A simple changing of the television channel or choosing not to enter a turnstile may be the best Christian response to a questionable Disney product—always being prepared, of course, to explain the convictions underlying our actions.
>
> Christians owe the nonbelieving public a little less action and a lot more thought. Believer-initiated boycotts have their place, but only when integrated into a biblical agenda of reconciliation between God and His people and between one another.[31]

Robert Knight suggests yet another problem:

> What happens when a company that

has a bad track record of being anti-Christian turns a bit, listens to the criticism, then turns out a product that is wholesome? Do you forgive and forget and support that product as a way of [encouraging] more of the same, or do you resist even that product until the company cleans up the rest of its act?[32]

Regrettably, Disney has shown no signs of returning to wholesomeness. We can pray and hope that the day will come. Meanwhile, there are the turnstiles that we do not need to enter. And the TV channel selectors that require our attention.

Endnotes

1. News Bulletin, July 31, 1995, Ab5wdrls, AOL.
2. "Disneyland's Gay Pride," *OC Weekly*, October 13-19, 1995, p. 10.
3. Ibid.
4. Ibid.
5. "Let's Boycott Disney," Associated Press On-line, p. 195.
6. AP Online, November 1995.
7. "Disney to Extend Benefits to Partners of Gays and Lesbians," *Herald-Tribune*, Sarasota, FL, October 8, 1995, p. 9B.
8. Steven Gaines, "Will the Mouse Come Out?," *Buzz Magazine*, May 1995, p. 9B.

9. Ibid.; *AFA Journal,* June 1995 (regarding Thomas Schumacher's sexual orientation).

10. *Buzz*, p. 9B.

11. Ibid.

12. Ibid.

13. Ibid.

14. Ibid.

15. Ibid.; Barbara Walters, *20/20*, November 11, 1994, quoted in *People Weekly,* November 14, 1994, vol. 42, no. 20, p. 4.

16. Stryker McGuire, "Yeah, So Sue Me," *Newsweek,* April 15, 1996, p. 77.

17. *Buzz*, p. 9B.

18. Michael Medved, *Hollywood vs. America* (New York, Harper Perennial, 1992), p. 310.

19. Ibid., p. 311.

20. Ibid., pp. 312-313.

21. *Buzz*, p. 9B.

22. Ibid.

23. *AFA Journal,* March 1996.

24. *Growing Up Gay in America,* press release by Lisa Kitei (New York: Hyperion, 1995).

25. Funny Gay Males, *Growing Up Gay in America* (New York: Hyperion, 1995), p. 2.

26. Hyperion press release on RuPaul (New York: Hyperion, 1995).

27. RuPaul, *Lettin' It All Hang Out* (New York: Hyperion, 1995), p. 1.

28. Ibid., p. 2.

29. Ibid., p. 79.

30. "News Bites," *Orange County* [Calif.] *Register,* August 23, 1995, p. Show-3.

31. Roberto Rivera, Editorial, *Christianity Today*, February 5, 1996, p. 13.

32. Robert Knight, Family Research Council, 1996, interview on file with author.

Epilogue

The motion picture still has great things ahead. Equipped with its big screens, its color and sound fidelities, and all its perfected devices for illusionment, absolutely nothing is beyond its range and powers.
— *Walt Disney*

Some Christians apparently feel that at least some of the anger exhibited against Disney for the change in its perceived direction and its embracement of in-your-face homosexuality is wrong. Some call it "superstitious Christianity."

For example, in an article by the same name in *Moody* magazine, author Quentin J. Schultze, draws some disturbing conclusions. He tells of an article in the *Wall Street Journal* about how a rumor spread about subliminal sex in Disney's *Aladdin,* tracing the "rumor" back through print to a prolife publication.

Schultze says that the rumor mill among Christians is fueled by fear:

> Scripture suggests that rumors, as a

form of public gossip, generally arise when fearful people are factious, arrogant, and deceitful (2 Corinthians 12:20; Romans 1:29). Fear leads us to look for simple answers to very complex questions, such as why people commit grotesque sins or why Hollywood produces violent and obscene entertainment. Fear seems to justify criticizing others.

Fearful Christians create partly true stories about real people and events. As the rumors circulate, we convince ourselves they must be true. Finally, Christian media publish or broadcast the rumors, convincing more people the rumors are accurate. Ignorance becomes fact.[1]

Schultze says a fund-raising consultant told him that many evangelical fund-raising experts have found that it's easier to elicit contributions by using scary half-truths. The consultant, according to Schultze, labeled it "Sound-bite Marketing."

"Finally, we should check our own faith in Christ," Schultze recommends concerning Christians accepting rumors. "Are we more excited about salvation by Jesus Christ or about the latest salvos fired by our favorite talk-show hosts and media critics? Which one is our real faith? Unless we control our own superstitiousness, rumors may become our religion."[2]

Some attempt to discount the rumors of subliminal imagery because they are linked to fundamentalist Christians—those who are referred to by *The Washington Post* as "largely poor, uneducated, and easy to command"—but are they true?

Knight says a thousand times yes. "It's not subliminal when in *The Little Mermaid*, a minister gets an erection while presiding over a wedding ceremony," he says. "It's right there in living color. And all one has to do is look at the jacket art in the same movie. The castle in the background contains a large phallus—much too realistic for anything subliminal. As a matter of fact, Disney has redesigned that cover."[3]

The first time the penis-like depiction was noticed was in July 1990, when Michelle Couch, of Mesa, Arizona complained to Disney and a Phoenix supermarket chain about the cover, which possibly could have been drawn at Disney.[4]

Further reports say that in *The Lion King*, for example, as Simba plops down on the ground, rising whisps of dust swirl around and are said to form the letters S-E-X. This phenomenon was discovered when a four-year-old boy noticed the letters appear and told his mother (or aunt) about it.

One mainstream editor says that Disney's transgressions are hardly subliminal. "The problem with subliminal sexual imagery in Disney products is the fact that the vulgar, sometimes sexual content in Disney productions is all too 'liminal' as it is," says Philip Terzian, associate editor of the *Providence Journal*. "Forget the hidden pictures or subtle exploitation; the preponderance of evidence is abundantly explicit."[5]

> It is bad enough for instance, that Michael Eisner and his Disney Imagineers have distorted the saga of Pocahontas—the twelve-year-old daughter of Chief Powhatan who befriended the English settlers in Virginia and, some years later, married John Rolfe and moved to London—into a mythical environmental impact statement, complete with political message.
>
> The pre-pubescent Pocahontas herself has been transformed into a bosomy, silken-haired babe, whose libido is awakened by a muscular, blow-dried Capt. John Smith. Great for small children: it gets them on the road to sexuality early.[6]

Some of Disney's most vocal critics also say that the film actually promotes New Age thought.

In *Pocahontas,* the title character's dead grandmother has been reincarnated as a large tree who urges Pocahontas to "listen to the spirits."[7]

Similarly, in a book/cassette combination from Walt Disney Records, entitled, *Disney's Pocahontas—Listen with Your Heart*, Pocahontas is sitting talking with her reincarnated grandmother Willow. Pocahontas says, "Grandmother Willow, what is my path? How am I ever going to find it?"

Grandmother Willow then responds. "All around you are spirits, child. They live in the earth, the water, the sky. If you listen, they will guide you."[8]

Movieguide magazine, published by the Christian Film and Television Commission, appears to be shocked, saying that the movie promotes "ecological spiritualism."[9]

Noted author and New Age expert, David Jeremiah, says that God did give people dominion over nature.

> In Genesis 1:28 [RSV], He [God] said, "Fill the earth and subdue it; and have dominion over the fish of the sea and over the birds of the air and over every living thing that moves upon the earth."
>
> However, the earth and all of nature belong to God, not for us to exploit, but as things borrowed or held in trust. Man's dominion is under God's dominion.[10]

In the new environmental spiritualism so promoted in *Pocahontas*, Mother Earth is to be worshiped. "The personification of the earth is known as the Gaia theory," says Jeremiah. "Gaia was the earth goddess of ancient Greek and Roman mythology—the earth mother. The term as it is used by enviro-worshippers today refers to an Eastern, pantheistic idea that the earth is the goddess."[11]

New Age ecological spiritualism, then, beckons to those who inhabit the earth. "The call is to enter into a holistic consciousness from which all peoples, all forms of life, all manner of universal manifestation are seen as interdependent aspects of one truth."[12]

But *Pocahontas* also seems to encourage the belief in spirit guides—ascended and transformed masters who guide, protect, nurture and answer all of our questions about who we are and where we're going.

Jeremiah opposes this view, intimating that there may very well be spiritual guides, but of what spirit? "Jesus is not an 'enlightened master,' " Jeremiah says. "He is the only begotten Son of God the Father. He was sent to earth, where He lived and taught, and died on the cross for our sins and then rose from the dead. If we believe in Him, we have eternal life."[13]

In addition to the weaving of white magic and New Age thinking into the movie, critics also point to gross inaccuracies in the storyline. In reality, Pocahontas converted to Christianity and was baptized, but there is no mention of this in the Disney version of her life.[14]

"They [Disney] seem to not just dislike Christians and their families, but despise them," says Alan Wildmon of the American Family Association.[15]

In addition to Disney's purported promotion of the "Goddess Earth" concept in *Pocahontas,* critics also point to the mega-hit Disney movie *The Lion King* as a flagrant furtherance of Buddhism.

Former Buddhist Jim Stephens is quoted as comparing the baboon named Rafiki, who seems to perform various forms of a religious ceremony throughout the movie, including anointing the baby lion, Simba, with dust from the earth, with Hindu asceticism.

> Rafiki is shown in a prayer posture called a "goma honza" of a double-lotus position which is used in meditation. People used to get really upset when they heard about movie houses planting suggestions in peoples' minds by flashing subliminal images of popcorn or soda on screens. Now Disney is putting images of Buddhism on the screen in viewers' faces, and people need to get upset and complain about it.[16]

> Thirty years ago Disney movies tended to involve flying rubber, Dean Jones, anthropomorphic cars and small-town misadventures. The closest thing to sex was a kiss for Fred MacMurray; the worst thing that could happen was to lose the big game. The children were childish and the adults were foolish.[17]

Now the adults are still foolish, but

the children are something like sullen ex-addicts. The [new Disney] movies are suffused with what might be called a New York sensibility: loud voices, foul-mouthed kids, witty references to flatulence . . . and so on.[18]

The Disney of the 1990s has been painted as a violator of family values by many Christians and Christian groups. They point to not only what the company has already done but what it continues to do.

Disney continues to host the annual "Gay & Lesbian Day" at Walt Disney World, complete with liquor and festivities, including a transvestite dance. An ad in *OUT* magazine urges gay goers to "pick up your Digital Queers Hospitality pack."[19]

Furthermore, Disney is rumored to be hard at work planning a New Age-style resort in Orlando where the enlightened set can attend workshops on self-discovery and "deeper exploration through contemplation, meditation, and centering," according to the brochure.[20]

Disney, though, is carrying the New Age theme into yet another planned movie called *Godspeak,* about a "god-conscious autistic adolescent named Erika. The film explores her relationship with a dolphin named Shanti, who acts as her therapist in bringing Erika closer to a higher reality."[21]

The continual injection of New Age consciousness in some of Disney's films prevails over Christian teachings. According to author and pastor, Dennis McCallum, New Age consciousness is an effort to affirm the good parts of all religions and develop a new meaning for spirituality. "Among other things," he says, "they argue that because humans are part of the cosmos, we are gods too. This is one reason contemporary spirituality focuses on the self, discovering our divinity within. New Age thinking is explicitly concerned with the journey toward realizing our essential divinity."[22]

The New Age has infiltrated Disney, it is supposed, but it has also seeped into ministries, medical offices and government agencies. Jeremiah, though, who says humanistic spirituality is filling America's religious void, gives solid advice when it comes to confronting the New Age. "If you can open your eyes to it, you can build a wall of fire around yourself to keep it from ever touching your life," he says.[23]

But what continues to touch the lives of countless Christians who have continued in their support of Disney is that organization's presumable hostility to anything Christian.

Disney, it seems, has dropped its seventeen-year-old "Glory and Pageantry of Christmas" presentation and has removed its nativity display. Reportedly, the company is favoring a generic "Holiday Festival," including Santa Claus, caroling and jazz renditions of Christmas music.[24]

New Age thought, homosexuality, Buddhism, black magic, occultism, Greek mythology, Satanism—it appears that Disney is the antithesis of everything Christians believe and hold dear.

But Disney's perceived obstinance, its worldly and anti-Christian bias has mobilized believers across the nation and beyond.

Film critic Michael Medved says the task of cleaning up the entertainment industry is great. "The struggle for the soul of the popular culture promises no quick or easy victories; all progress will be measured in subtle increments.

"Nevertheless, the battle has been joined and the groundwork is there for new offensives."[25]

Endnotes

1. Quentin J. Schultze, "Superstitious Christianity," *Moody*, March/April 1996, p. 39.

2. Ibid.

3. Robert Knight, Family Research Council, 1996, interview on file with author.

4. Internet: Newsprint 2.1, Openwin library 3, root@WMM, December 1995.

5. Philip Terzia, "Disney Transgressions Are Hardly Subliminal," *Patriot News* (Harrisburg, PA), November 28, 1995, p. A7.

6. Ibid.

7. Dave Geisler, "Christians Launch Disney Boycott," *Charisma*, October 1995, p. 31.

8. *Disney's Pocahontas: Listen with Your Heart* (Orlando, FL: Walt Disney Company, 1995), p. 5.

9. Matt Kline, *Movieguide Magazine*, vol. 10, #14, July "A," 1995, p. 8, quoted in Dave Geisler, "Chris-

tians Launch Disney Boycott," *Charisma*, October 1995, p. 31.

10. David Jeremiah, *Invasion of Other Gods* (Dallas TX: Word, 1995), p. 155.

11. Ibid., p. 169.

12. Barry McWaters, *Conscious Evolution: Personal and Planetary Transformation* (Los Angeles: New Age Press, 1981), foreword, quoted in ibid., p. 160.

13. Ibid., p. 150.

14. *Charisma*, p. 31.

15. Personal interview with Alan Wildmon. Notes on file with author.

16. Ibid.

17. *Patriot News*, p. A7.

18. Ibid.

19. Advertisement in the homosexual publication, *OUT* magazine, featuring Mickey Mouse's ears, June 1995.

20. *Vogue*, September 1995, p. 172.

21. Ibid.

22. David McCallum, *The Death of Truth* (Minneapolis, MN: Bethany House, 1996), p. 208.

23. Jeremiah, p. 155.

24. AFA press release, December 7, 1995.

25. Michael Medved, *Hollywood vs. America* (New York: Harper Perennial, 1992), p. 345.

Where Do We Go from Here?

You have just read some startling information offered, not by an eccentric doomsday prophet, but by a respected investigative reporter. His documentation demonstrates that Disney is a major force propelling America to the precipice of cultural destruction.

The facts are clear:

- Biblically based family values are attacked;

- Occultism, Satanism, Eastern religions and New Age philosophy are promoted;

- Sexual perversion is modeled and applauded as an acceptable alternative lifestyle.

- Consumer demands are not only being satisfied, they are being generated and created.

All of these trends, tendencies, policies and agendas fly in the face of Scripture.

For some, the impact of this material will be no less than seismic. The "kick in the gut" delivered by the final chapter is infinitely distressing. The question must be asked: What will you do about what you have read?

The temptation is to choose to be passive, to nod in empathy with the author, bemoan America's sad moral state and then forget the warning.

That choice has a smugness about it which betrays an underlying apathy for the welfare of people, especially little people, who are being subtly but surely pulled into the stewpot of moral decay which is American culture.

The problems *Disney and the Bible* present cannot be ignored. One of the "pillars" of American culture, which formerly represented decency and innocence, is crumbling.

Question. Does entertainment itself need to be questioned?

> For centuries the Church stood solidly against every form of worldly entertainment, recognizing it for what it was—a device for wasting time, a refuge from the disturbing voice of conscience, a scheme to divert attention from moral accountability. For this she got herself abused roundly by the sons of this world. But of late she has become tired of the abuse and has given over the struggle.[1]

Is Disney of absorbing interest to Christians these days only because the false god of entertainment has been given credence in the first place? Is all this being discussed because the Church has sold out?

Consider some of those principles:

- ***Do not be squeezed into the world's mold.***

  I beseech you therefore, brethren, by the mercies of God, that ye present your bodies a living sacrifice, holy, acceptable unto God, which is your reasonable service. And be not conformed to this world: but be ye transformed by the renewing of your mind, that ye may prove what is that good, and acceptable, and perfect, will of God. (Romans 12:1-2)

- ***Sanctify yourselves to avoid outer and inner contamination.***

  Wherefore come out from among them, and be ye separate, saith the Lord, and touch not the unclean thing; and I will receive you, and will be a Father unto you, and ye shall be my sons and daughters, saith the Lord Almighty. Having therefore these promises, dearly beloved, let us cleanse ourselves from all filthiness of the flesh and spirit, perfecting holiness in the fear of God. (2 Corinthians 6:17-18; 7:1)

- ***Focus on what is good and godly.***

  Finally, brethren, whatsoever things are true, whatsoever things are honest, whatsoever things are just, whatsoever things are pure, whatsoever things are lovely, whatsoever things are of good report; if there be any virtue, and if there be any praise, think on these things. (Philippians 4:8)

- ***Flee evil, follow righteousness.***

  Flee also youthful lusts: but follow righteousness, faith, charity, peace, with them that call on the Lord out of a pure heart. (2 Timothy 2:22)

- ***Be innocent about evil.***

  I would have you wise unto that which is good, and simple concerning evil. (Romans 16:19b)

Action. These Scriptures demand some practical responses. Truth requires action! Christian action is always based on the teaching and principles of the Bible which are the believer's guide in all matters of life and conduct. For the concerned and caring Christian, the following options offer redemptive potential and yes, spiritual power:

- Align yourself with the sentiments of those who are speaking out against Disney for godly reasons.

- Write letters of protest.

- Choose carefully which Disney products, if any, to purchase.

- Cut off financial support by refusing to frequent Disney movies and theme parks.

- Pray for wisdom and discernment for yourself and your children.

- Pray for our nation's moral state which so easily permits perversity and degradation.

- Pray for Disney, especially for its leadership.

Finally, there are two basic biblical ideas which clarify the big picture and help us to respond in appropriate ways:

1. Understand that evil is contagious. The Bible likens evil to yeast (1 Corinthians 5:6-7) which enlarges and permeates the whole. There need be no further documentation that unrestrained evil, especially through films and television, is spreading exponentially throughout the fabric of American society. It is spreading, in part, through Disney.

2. Understand that judgment always comes. Biblical history is linear—it is going somewhere, and there is an end in view. The Scriptures, particularly the Old Testament, reveal moral

decline, corruption and destruction. Always judgment comes. America is on its way. It is heading to destruction, energized, again in part, by the Disney empire.

Thankfully, there is hope. The Bible also promises that when the enemy (Satan and those he influences) comes in like a flood, the Lord will raise an opposing standard against him (Isaiah 59:19).

Pendulums do swing. If this book becomes even a small part of a resolute resistance which eventually leads to moral renewal in America, we will be grateful.

The Publishers
August 1996

Endnote

1. A.W. Tozer, *The Root of the Righteous* (Camp Hill, PA: Christian Publications, 1986), p. 32.

Other Horizon Books
in this Popular Apologetics
and the Bible™ series:

Rush Limbaugh and the Bible

Embraced by the Light and the Bible

The Less Traveled Road and the Bible